PRAISE FOR UNTIL IT'S GONE

A great blend of idealistic and practical, sensible and world-changing. I hope every community leader in America reads this book. I am ready to work for a Circles Campaign in my community.

– Mary Pipher, author of bestselling *Reviving Ophelia*

It is critical that the issues of the environment and of poverty be linked together in our minds and actions because they are inextricably connected in the world. Scott Miller connects the dots between the two and offers practical steps that each of us can take to address both of these challenges together.

– Carolyn Raffensperger, environmental attorney, co-editor of *Precautionary Tools for Reshaping Environmental Policy*

Scott Miller is one who dreams and makes those dreams a reality through dedicated work, integrity, commitment, and unsquelchable enthusiasm. In Miller, poverty has a formidable adversary.

– Arleen Lorrance, MFA, co-founder of Teleos Institute, Artistic Director of The Theatre of Life, author of *The Love Principles*

This book provides a vision that poverty could actually be eradicated from our society. It provides a structure proven to be workable and successful, and offers each caring person hope, inspiration, and impetus to get to work "until it's gone."

– Diane Kennedy Pike, MA, consciousness coach, co-director of Teleos Institute, author of *Life as a Waking Dream* and *House of Self*

You are going to smile when you read this book. Scott Miller is direct, refreshing, and challenging. Once you shift paradigms, you'll discover the joy that underlies this work.

– Phillip E. DeVol, co-author of *Bridges Out of Poverty* and author of *Getting Ahead in a Just-Gettin'-By World*

If we are to have community sustainability, then we must address issues of economic justice. That can only occur when there are relationships of mutual respect between and among the classes. Scott Miller identifies the process that allows those relationships to develop. The process he has identified is pure genius. It is a tool that individuals in poverty need in order to make a transition and also allows individuals from middle class and wealth to understand poverty.

– Ruby K. Payne, author of bestselling *A Framework for Understanding Poverty* and co-author of *Bridges Out of Poverty*

Until It's Gone *shines clarity and optimism on a situation that generally is regarded as hopeless. Miller not only gives us insight into factors contributing to poverty, but provides a roadmap for transformation of individuals and communities called the Circles Campaign. No reader is left wondering, "But what can I do?" Miller asks the hard questions and then provides solutions for ending poverty in this nation.*

– David Heitmiller and Jacque Blix, co-authors of *Getting a Life*

For the great strides we as a nation have made in technology, medicine, and education, it is appalling that we have not figured out how to help our own people meet their basic needs. This book will give you hope and guide you in the right direction to start making a change.

– Julie Bradley, Circle Leader

Until It's Gone

ENDING POVERTY IN OUR NATION, IN OUR LIFETIME

Introducing Circles™, a national campaign of support, training, and opportunity

Scott C. Miller

CO-FOUNDER
MOVE THE MOUNTAIN LEADERSHIP CENTER

Scott C. Miller
Until It's Gone: Ending Poverty In Our Nation, In Our Lifetime, 166 pp.
Bibliography pp. 141–143
ISBN 10: 1-934583-01-4
ISBN 13: 978-1-934583-01-2
1. Social Welfare 2. Community Action 3. Title

Published by aha! Process, Inc.

Personal stories compiled by Darci Kellen
Content and copy editing by Mary Conrad Lo
Text design by Sara Patton
Printed in the United States of America

Library of Congress: 2007926840

This book is dedicated to the memory of my father,
Charles L. Miller.

A talented writer with a great sense of humor and an intelligent, affable leader from an early age, he challenged the status quo and inspired me to do the same. I learned from his example to honor work not only as a source of income, but also as a source of purpose and meaning. He provided consistent financial security while teaching me the wisdom of "having enough." Because of his life, I understand I can control my destiny and make a difference in the world.

Contents

Acknowledgments

I wish to thank Gary Stokes, the co-founder of Move the Mountain Leadership Center, for the thousands of hours of dialogue we have had over the past 20 years. These conversations have been vital for formulating the theories and strategies presented in this book.

To my spiritual mentors, Arleen Lorrance and Diane Pike: I am grateful for your constant inspiration and for your insights into what it means to be a transformational leader.

To Lois Smidt, who co-founded Beyond Welfare with me: Thank you for your partnership in bringing something new and of value into the world. Your understanding of what it takes to build relationships with people from different backgrounds and walks of life is as deep as your commitment to pursuing them.

Many thanks to Julie Bradley and her children, Russell and Nicole, and to Noumoua Lynalou and her daughter, Arabesque, for leading me as an ally in your Circles of support. Both of your families have provided me with the opportunity to give, as well as receive. Your patience with me as I learn how to be an effective ally is most appreciated.

To my colleagues, Eileen Wallace, Michelle Clark, Gena Atcher, and Mary Sigmann: Thank you for your reliable, intelligent, humorous, and encouraging partnership. You comprise an amazing team for our work. And a big thanks to all of the wonderful community leaders who have taken up the mantle of ending poverty. We have learned much from joining with you fabulous people.

My collaborators at aha! Process, Inc.—Peggy Conrad in publications and my editor, Mary C. Lo—have been terrific. Your fine work transformed a compilation of essays into a coherent and compelling manuscript.

To Darci Kellen: Thank you for doing such an excellent job of interviewing Circle allies and writing up stories about the families they are supporting. I also want to thank Jody Clark and Mary Sigmann for their early editing contributions to the manuscript.

To my mom, who has always been my best ally: I want to thank you for giving me what I needed growing up so that I could think independently and creatively about my work. To my brothers and sister and their families: Thanks for being interested in what I do for a living and remaining a close extended family.

And to my wife, Jan: Thanks for all the endless conversations that have enabled me to take the next step and the next . . . We have had more than our fair share of middle-of-the-night "seminars" after I woke up realizing that, once again, I was in over my head trying to learn how to make things work.

– Scott C. Miller
May 2007

Note from the Author

The headline of the national news section in this morning's *Des Moines Register* says, "U.S. severe poverty rate is worst since '75." A family of four having an annual income of less than $9,903—*half* the federal poverty standard—was considered "severely poor" in 2005: nearly 16 million United States citizens fall into this category.

An analysis of the 2005 census done by the McClatchy Newspapers found that the number of "severely poor" rose 26% from 2000 to 2005. "... Worker productivity has increased dramatically since the brief recession of 2001, but wages and job growth lagged behind. At the same time, the share of national income going to corporate profits has dwarfed the amount going to wages and salaries ... it also suggests that social programs aren't as effective as they once were at catching those who fall into economic despair."

There is clearly a moral imperative to end poverty, but what would be the economic and societal impact of achieving such a goal? Recently, The Center for American Progress produced a report titled "The Economic Costs of Poverty" (based on research conducted at the University of Chicago, Northwestern University, Georgetown University, and the Urban Institute). The report concludes that the cost to our nation of having children raised in poverty is $500B (*billion*) a year! Ending poverty is a moral, economic, *and* social imperative.

Can we end poverty in this nation? According to the U.S. Census Bureau, the lowest level we have officially reached since keeping records was 11.1% in 1973. In 2005, it was 12.6%. Having worked in the field for over 25 years, it is clear to me that unless a public will to end this situation intervenes, poverty levels probably will continue to grow. This public will must be fueled by ordinary citizens like you and me who are willing to communicate effectively and insistently to our neighbors, as well as to our political leaders. The trend is for the gulf between "the rich" and "the poor" to continue widening, a trend that ultimately endangers our democracy. I, for one, am not willing to let this happen without doing what I can to suggest an alternate route.

One pathway out of poverty that I present in this book is the Circles™ Campaign alternative. It's a way of surrounding a family in poverty with ongoing support. Several individuals in poverty who have been in a Circle—along with supportive allies—have been kind enough to share their real-life stories in the pages of this book. All names have been changed in order to protect confidentiality.

Moving beyond poverty as a nation will require each of us who share such a vision to *become the change we want to see happen*, to paraphrase Mahatma Gandhi. By examining your own life's choices, attitudes, and beliefs, you too can align the personal forces that are available to you toward the task of eliminating poverty. It is within the grasp of each of us to unleash enormous power to transform our society so that one day no one will ever have to live in poverty again.

I wrote this book to inspire and equip you to become a more powerful ally and advocate for families who suffer in poverty. Poverty is a condition that *we can eradicate* when enough public compassion and will combine with widespread clarity and effective leadership. Contact us anytime at www.movethemountain.org for help with getting started in your own community.

Scott C. Miller
Move the Mountain Leadership Center
416 Douglas St., Suite 205
Ames, IA 50010
(515) 232-9285
scott@movethemountain.org

Until It's Gone

ENDING POVERTY IN OUR NATION, IN OUR LIFETIME

PART I

Reframing the Problem of Poverty

To eliminate poverty, what's needed is a consciously made collective decision that there is no longer any need for it to exist: a societal paradigm shift. *We must agree that it is not necessary for the well-being of any nation that some of us work for less than a living wage —that some individuals live in poverty while working as hard as anyone else, often at jobs considered undesirable by most.*

When we examine attitudes prevalent in the United States, we find there's broad acceptance of the belief that if people work hard and play by the rules, they should be able to meet basic needs and have some money left over to invest for the future. This belief can form a foundation for developing new, improved public policies and novel social contracts between and among local, state, and national governments and individuals. This is an important next step toward building a more equitable society. Still, the most significant work needed lies in the realm of making a personal shift from seeking happiness outside of ourselves toward finding happiness within— and toward the experience of living in closer community with others. This crucial shift in mindset will compel us to develop new goals for our systems, such as the complete eradication of poverty. Having goals like this will result in new social and political norms and, ultimately, in the construction of a more just, more inclusive civilization.

CHAPTER 1

Not 'Reduce' Poverty—*End* Poverty

Framing our work in terms of "ending poverty" rather than "reducing poverty" keeps us from colluding with the assumption that it's acceptable to have *some* poverty—from thinking that we are incapable of building a society without poverty. Is *some* poverty acceptable? No more than *some* racism, *some* cancer, or *some* gang violence—*some* shootings in *some* school buildings or *some* terrorism in *some* states. As a matter of fact, poverty exacerbates these problems, along with many others like them. Millions of people living in poverty die younger than they need to from preventable diseases. Far too many are depressed and demoralized by conditions that may have existed throughout their entire lives. Too often, when listening to public dialogue, led for the most part by public officials, we are left with the impression that poverty is not that big a problem. But poverty is a national *emergency* and needs to be viewed as such.

These disturbing facts, together with our personal experiences of relating to people living without enough, motivated us at Move the Mountain Leadership Center to identify and pursue ideas that might re-engage individual communities in the process of responding more effectively to local poverty. Hurricane Katrina temporarily lifted consciousness and dialogue to a more appropriate level nationwide. Now we need to work to reinstate and sustain that same kind of focused awareness.

> Before Joan's* husband died, he had been a semi-invalid for two and a half years. "When he was alive . . . I had to work because of the insurance. His drug bill without insurance was $500 to $600 a month."

* All names used in the personal stories included in this book have been changed.

> Twenty years earlier, he had destroyed three discs in his lower back, so Joan had been the breadwinner that whole time. She worked five to six days a week, 10 to 12 hours a day. "After I would work overtime like that, I would feel so drug down and felt like I didn't have anything or anybody. When he got sick, all of our friends seemed to drift away. They just didn't want to be bothered with us." Joan's life involved going to work and then coming home to find stacks of laundry to do, supper to cook, a house to clean . . . and then she was up two or three times a night to help her husband. "The pace really wore me down. It took everything out of me."

MOVE THE MOUNTAIN LEADERSHIP CENTER

In 1992, as Move the Mountain began to define a group of working theories, we learned that it's the mindset prevalent among those involved at the highest levels of strategizing that determines which goals ultimately are set for a community. As a result, beginning in 1995 we put our full attention into producing leadership-development tools. Since then, Move the Mountain has been helping community leaders in education, human services, and other fields to better articulate their various goals and develop more intentional sets of strategies for implementing their plans. Soon it became clear to us that social-service agencies can reach only a small portion of the population living in poverty. In addition, such agencies (for the most part) can provide only limited, temporary services. Our nation's network of anti-poverty agencies seems somehow to have become one focused more on grants management than on effective action strategies for engaging communities locally.

Responsibility for ending poverty rests with every individual as we interact in federal, state, and local governments; in business communities; in our neighborhoods and faith communities; and in our families.

No single individual *or group* can be expected to assume responsibility for the entire task of ending poverty. Move the Mountain's mission is to inspire and equip thousands of *transformational leaders* and thousands of other groups to work toward the goal of ending poverty.

THE CIRCLES™ MODEL

One strategy we've implemented is called the *Circles Campaign.*

> After her husband died, Joan was at a low point in her life. She lived in senior housing far from town. It was extremely hard on her that she couldn't go many places, and the loneliness really got to her. "I don't think I would be around today if I didn't get in with Circles."

A Circle comprises two, three, or more volunteers—"Circle allies"—who meet monthly with the head(s) of a single family—"Circle leader(s)"—to seek solutions for the daily problems, large and small, faced by those wanting to get out of poverty. Groups of Circle leaders meet together weekly to share a meal and a program. Major focus is placed on improving self-sufficiency, expanding social networks, and enhancing academic performance of both children and parents.

In each community, Move the Mountain's goal is to provide a strong foundation for Circles in order to ensure that useful knowledge gained from experience is embedded into this ongoing process, and that unique talents, interests, strengths, and insights available are utilized to the fullest.

The Circles Campaign is a *high-impact strategy,* which means that it can:

- Change the mindset of a community so that ending poverty becomes a desired outcome.
- Change current policies and approaches to ending poverty.
- Empower people in poverty to help solve *community* problems as they work to achieve financial independence.

High impact strategies are actions taken to move from the current reality of pervasive poverty to a *preferred future,* which describes a time when individuals and families have become economically self-sufficient. Through Circles, people can find reasons, relationships, and the resources necessary to thrive.

Beginning a Circles Campaign is a very practical way to build a new, broad-based constituency around the agenda of ending poverty. It's a simple idea that has captured the imagination of politicians, faith leaders, neighborhood organizers, social workers, educators, and business leaders across the United States. A team of people supports members of one family as they work their way out of poverty. Although the process of helping a family out of poverty is complex, the concept of Circles is not, making it attractive for many.

Participating in a Circle gives anyone—public officials included—a new opportunity to get close to the pain of poverty by sharing the experience of one family. Working together in an organized way, systemic barriers to moving out of poverty can be addressed.

The deeper motive underlying the Circles Campaign is to invite everyone to consider making changes that stem from enhanced generosity and compassion —and to develop simpler lifestyles that are more sustainable and enjoyable. As one makes friends with people who have extremely limited financial resources, it becomes more difficult to spend money frivolously. As we engage in intentional dialogue about poverty and its causes, we often recognize that a simpler lifestyle would reduce anxiety and bring a stronger sense of meaning and peace to our lives. Our need to over-consume—to accumulate possessions to fill emotional needs—diminishes. We begin to see the world around us in new ways, which can stimulate an interest in advocating for new, more equitable social and public policies.

THE NATIONAL CIRCLES CAMPAIGN

With the help of federal funding, we brought Move the Mountain into communities in Arizona, California, Connecticut, Idaho, Indiana, Iowa, Minnesota, Missouri, Nebraska, Nevada, New Mexico, Ohio, Pennsylvania, and Vermont. As of early 2007 more than 30 organizations were working with us to develop the Circles Campaign. We recently began collaborating with Dr. Ruby K. Payne, author of *A Framework for Understanding Poverty*, and Phil DeVol, author of *Getting Ahead in a Just-Gettin'-By World* and co-author with Dr. Payne and Terie Dreussi Smith of *Bridges Out of Poverty*, on this initiative.

We will track the journeys of families in communities across the nation as they work to leave poverty. As the Circles Campaign unfolds, we will be able to answer the questions, "What does it take for people to get out of poverty in this country?" and "What would it take for us as a nation to include all our people in our collective prosperity?" in more comprehensive, realistic ways.

HIDDEN RULES AND MENTAL MODELS

In order for individuals who have been raised in different socioeconomic circumstances to build effective relationships, it's very helpful to be able to use "mental models" as guides. Dr. Payne clearly describes significant cultural differences among those having low, middle, and high incomes, a phenomenon she has called "the hidden rules of class." These hidden rules help explain why people typically tend to continue living in the same economic circumstances in which they were raised.

Understanding these ideas can give people a greater awareness of limitations imposed by their own upbringing—and can provide tools for expanding options through utilization of certain cultural norms of those earning significantly different incomes. This can be especially useful for low-income earners who want to succeed in mainstream educational and corporate institutions. It also can be helpful for people with middle and upper incomes who want to infuse their lives with more meaning and diminish the stress connected with relentlessly pursuing more money.

Incorporating Dr. Payne's insights into our Circles Campaigns provides Circle leaders and allies a fresh orientation and a new language for more successfully negotiating their new relationships. People become more patient and understanding after realizing that, as in any relationship involving different cultures, hidden rules are often unknowingly broken. Once such hidden rules—assumptions and attitudes—are acknowledged and discussed, people can learn, forgive, teach, heal, and move on.

■ ■ ■

I believe that as long as we are caught up in wanting more "stuff" and status to make us feel good rather than in becoming more purposeful about expanding our consciousness, we will continue to come up short in having enough personal power to effect significant, transformational change. Anyone, however, who passionately pursues a mission that is aligned with his or her own inner purpose can have a profound impact on family, community, and society in general. He or she can *move mountains*. The purpose of our organization is to seek out these individuals and provide them with support through our speaking, consulting, executive coaching, training, and technical assistance programs: our national community of Circles Campaigns.

Joan found out about Circles from a friend. "I went and enjoyed the company, and it got me out of the house every week." She kept showing up at the meetings and made some valuable connections. "There were some ladies that were allies, and they worked at the career center, and I said that I wanted a part-time job. I know that at 60 not too many people want to hire you, but they told me about a program that sets people up with jobs. I got hired in and have worked ever since, and I really love it." She works in the Salvation Army thrift store and looks forward to helping people each day.

Joan really struggled with transportation, but through Circles she was able to find some help. "There were very few buses that would come out here for church. One of my allies would come out to drive me there. If I didn't have that help, I would be stuck at my house, and it was really a bad day for me knowing I couldn't go anywhere." After working with her allies for several months, they figured out how to get a car for her. This was a life-changing event, bringing a real sense of freedom she didn't have before.

Joan is continuing to make changes with the help of her allies. "I'm trying to save a little bit of money. One of my allies is helping me budget." She has saved some money now, something that had not been possible for a long time. "When my husband was sick, about everything I worked for went to living expenses and medicine."

TODAY IS THE DAY

A nation's move into a more responsible, conscious, and compassionate society is by no means inevitable. It is a choice that must be made by enough individuals, each willing to make our world better for everyone.

As Dr. Martin Luther King Jr. reminded us in the '60s, "We are now faced with the fact that tomorrow is today. We are confronted with the fierce urgency of now. In this unfolding conundrum of life and history, there is such a thing as being too late."

The words "ending poverty" need to come to the forefront of our collective national consciousness. The mindset within our individual communities must change to allow for social strategies that can become big enough to get the entire job done. As a national—and, ultimately, world—community, we need to stop normalizing the existence of poverty in the midst of wealth. We need to challenge our own personal assumptions about what is and is not possible. We need to believe that people in poverty who want to get out can do so when given enough opportunity and support. We must insist that everyone deserves to be supported while becoming prepared to participate in our country's unprecedented prosperity. We need to believe that middle- and upper-income earners will choose lifestyles that contribute to a more sustainable society and a healthier environment—lifestyles that will help eradicate poverty. Poverty *can* be dismantled. That is the message that needs to be communicated to people sympathetic to the plight of those living without enough—to those able to see the connection between their own well-being and the well-being of everyone.

In every community where I've spoken, audiences become enthusiastic about forming Circles. Circles offer immediate, hands-on, manageable steps anyone can take along the path toward solving the larger complex dynamics of poverty. People appreciate the invitation to become personally involved. Translating the message that poverty can be *dismantled* into meaningful action brings us all closer to a future in which *every person* will be able to lead a fulfilling, productive life.

Through the support she has received, Joan is now giving back to other families in Circles. "I go and pick up a couple of families that don't have transportation and take them to the Circles meeting. I try to do what I can with people and try to be helpful." She feels like she really is a part of a community of people and tries to be as giving as she can in many areas of her life. She attended leadership seminars in her church, and helped in a walk for poverty. "I walked four miles that day and everyone was shocked I could do that. I was proud of myself."

CHAPTER 2

Building Circles

WHO SUPPORTS CIRCLES?

At the time of this writing, Move the Mountain is working with more than 30 communities that are coming together to establish Circles Campaigns. In each community, a transformational leader working through a *lead organization* builds a Guiding Coalition that consists of community members and representatives of established social services organizations, faith organizations, schools, grassroots groups, and/or housing initiatives. The lead organization provides two staff people to support the Guiding Coalition as it develops the Circles Campaign. Teams are formed to raise resources, recruit and train volunteers to act as allies, hold weekly meetings, and generally raise public awareness in order to build momentum for finding large-scale solutions to poverty.

You will recall that a Circle is a group of two to five people—"Circle allies"—who make a commitment to help the head(s) of one family—"Circle leader(s)"—out of poverty. They meet together as a team at least once a month to focus on both long- and short-term goals that will help members of the leader family find their way out of poverty. The Circle leader is trained and supported to lead the group, as well as to ask allies for specific help with specific needs. Allies are free to help each other in any way that makes sense to the Circle and are discouraged from taking on assignments they don't actively want. Helpful assignments can include finding a donated car or computer; helping write a résumé; coaching a family member about getting into the workforce; or joining family members on important appointments related to education, work, or necessary support services. Allies also can provide financial donations to a revolving loan program targeted for a particular family's self-sufficiency plan. (Circles policy is that any decision to give or loan money needs to be made with input from at least one other ally, and that the issue of whether it's a gift or a loan be clearly understood by all involved. Terms for repayment need to be articulated unambiguously at the time a loan is made: In some cases, this has taken the form of providing a specified number of hours of volunteer service in the community.)

Friends of Circle allies can offer to any number of Circle leaders specific help, such as repairing computers, networking people to jobs, offering car repair services, or providing clothing. There are limitless ways in which an ally can help a family with the practical steps necessary to move out of poverty.

The key to success lies in the various ways that Circle leaders and their allies are supported, not just within the individual Circle, but also by trained staff who provide orientation sessions, regular support sessions, and a phone number for anyone involved to call when help is needed. Circle allies do whatever they can to help without being expected to rescue, fix, or interfere inappropriately with the decision-making rights and responsibilities of the leaders they are supporting. In addition, leader families leaving poverty support one another in weekly sessions facilitated by the trained staff members.

BIG VIEW MEETINGS

Each month all Circle leaders and allies are invited to a "Big View" meeting to organize actions aimed at educating the broader community about barriers faced by families as they move out of poverty. Big View meetings are held to share successes and roadblocks, as well as to serve as forums for addressing major relevant issues.

Big View meetings can help mobilize an entire community to pursue seriously an end to poverty. The Governor of Iowa spoke at the first large Des Moines Circles Big View Conference. His son, an attorney and Circle member, had taken his commitment to the Circles approach home to his parents. Legislators, school superintendents, college presidents, police chiefs, welfare directors, and numerous other community leaders have attended Big View meetings to learn directly from people living in poverty about struggles faced and how to help.

BUILDING A CIRCLES COMMUNITY

What truly helps families find a way out of poverty is to become part of a community of people with different socioeconomic backgrounds who have learned to care about one another. We've learned over the years that achieving this situation in a community requires the implementation of a number of steps, including:

1. **Defining a common vision** of ending poverty for everyone to work toward.
2. **Defining a common language** to discuss similarities and differences. We use aha! Process' books and training sessions to teach people about Dr. Payne's "hidden rules of class." Circle allies read and learn from *Bridges Out of Poverty* and Circle leaders use *Getting Ahead in a Just-Getting'-By World.*
3. **Defining a shared set of values** and principles to guide the healthy development of the community.
4. **Establishing an atmosphere of permission to use common sense,** so that people feel free to do whatever is most appropriate to solve particular problems and reach defined goals.
5. **Holding regularly scheduled meetings** to share and learn together. Weekly meetings of Circle leaders include a free meal and childcare to make it easier to attend.

CIRCLES ARE A FORCE FOR SOCIETAL CHANGE

Circles are intended to inspire and inform larger shifts in community programs and policies. Each Circle is focused on helping one family get completely out of poverty. When working toward this goal, the world comes into new focus. Barriers within established systems are revealed when short-term, fragmented objectives exclusive to single programs fail to meet the entire set of challenges a family faces on their journey. The primary question for a Circles Campaign to pose is: "What does it take to get out of poverty in this community, in this state, in this country, at this time?"

Harold is a passionate man who feels that the Circles Campaign has completely changed his view of poverty. "You can't go through an experience of Circles and say that it hasn't changed you. I'm not a soft-hearted person to start with, but that doesn't mean that I can't see how to help other people to get better and improve their lives." Harold became involved in Circles after he was elected County Commissioner. "I looked at this program saying, 'This isn't a program where we throw money at the problem; this is a program where we try to solve problems in a different fashion.' And that immediately perked my interest."

Involvement with Circles has really changed how Harold understands people living in poverty. "My attitude toward poor people was that they were uneducated, lazy people." After he started working with his family, he found out that they were as hard-working as he was. "They are better educated than I am, but they're in a set of circumstances that they can't get out of." He has come to appreciate the problems that his family has to face. "If I had to live on their income and live the way they do, I couldn't, so I have to really respect how they are getting by in life, and I have to respect that they don't want to live that way either."

When Harold first started in Circles, he thought that it would be easy to get people out of poverty. "I looked at this as a project—that I was going to get these people out of this very quickly." He discovered that finances aren't the only problem people have to deal with. "It's all the other issues they have in their lives, not just money; that may have been the hardest thing for me to realize." The longer Harold was in Circles, the more he understood his role as an ally. "I realized that this isn't a project, this is a family that I am trying to help through a hard situation or a time period in their life."

Harold has seen a lot of change in the family he's been working with. "They have realized that there are better things in life, and I don't mean that they are all purely financial." As members of a Circle, they have worked on getting out of survival mode into long-range plans. "The problem is that it isn't just about finances for them; it's their whole way of looking at life." The allies encourage their family to examine their talents and skills to help with self-esteem and self-worth issues. They have also looked at what goals would be most beneficial. One of the goals his family has made is to start putting money aside so their kids can have college educations and try to move out of the cycle of poverty. "I'm not saying we're 100% successful, but, man, we've made some small changes that have really helped."

Harold spreads his passion for Circles and encourages others to get started. "It all really comes back to looking into the kids' eyes, knowing that their parents aren't making a lot of money. If that doesn't tear at your heart strings, there is nothing in the world that will—especially when you're talking to people that are good parents, working as hard as they can and just struggling to get ahead in life." Being in a Circle is one way Harold is consciously trying to make a difference. "I'm approaching 50, so I looked back on life and decided that helping others is what it's all about. When I was in my 20s it was about making money; when I was in my 30s it was about raising kids; and now I'm in my late 40s, and I want to know how I'm going to impact the world." Harold doesn't look at Circles as a job; he looks at it as a way to really make an impact on someone's life.

For a summary of the processes required to start a Circles Campaign in your community, see pages 125–131.

PART II

Getting Our Priorities Straight

I have often wondered why, as a nation of communities, we tend to focus more attention on questions like how to expand new housing development to the southwest or to the north than on how to make sure that every child in our local school has enough food to eat, a solid roof for shelter, adequate clothing, and a nurturing adult presence in his or her life.

Maybe we think these problems are already being adequately addressed.

Unfortunately, for the most part, they are not.

So . . . how do we go about setting priorities in our communities? And why, even in the world's most affluent nations, is poverty such a persistent problem?

CHAPTER 3

Transformation Is Needed

There are societal *and* individual reasons for the fact that there are high levels of poverty in the U.S. According to a recent study by the well-respected Manpower Research Development Corporation, the poverty level has not decreased since 1973, mainly because of stagnation in earned income and an increase in the number of single-parent households. To reduce and eventually eliminate poverty from our communities, we have to work at solutions that address both societal problems (like providing livable wages) and individual challenges (like building and maintaining healthy relationships).

One of the largest common denominators for those living in poverty is *social isolation.* How does this happen? On the larger societal level, one of the many reasons for this is that people with adequate and more-than-adequate incomes simply don't mingle with people with low incomes, and vice versa. It's too uncomfortable. Feelings of guilt arise. So we keep our distance and retreat into denial and rationalization. Because of this social compartmentalization, a popular denial is that there *is* no poverty in my community, or, if there is, then those people are getting what they deserve. They shouldn't be allowed to have children if they're poor. People in poverty are lazy, they're drug users, they're spiritually ill—they're troublemakers who can't hold down a job.

Diane got involved in a Circles Campaign after she lost her job. "It was a union position, so I got laid off because I was the lowest on the totem pole." She found herself waiting tables and decided that joining a Circle would be a good opportunity. "I just felt a lot of shame. I think anybody in poverty does feel it because I worked really hard, am really smart, am a good person, but I still just can't make it." Diane was able to get a group of allies who were supportive in relation to what she needed. She got a job a couple of months later because there was a position opening up where she had previously worked. "I started working full time making $12 an hour by commuting an hour each way. So it was a lot of hours, but I knew there was light at the end of the tunnel, if I put in this time and had this experience. I was earning more money."

Diane remained very committed to her Circles group even after she got a job. "I would drive an hour to work, work for eight hours, drive an hour home to get my kids, and we would drive about another 45 minutes to get to Circles." They were really long days, but Diane knew the meetings offered her opportunities for leadership, and it was something they did together as a family. Her kids really looked forward to going because they made friends at the meetings. Diane made friends with her allies and gained some leadership skills, which she wouldn't have had the opportunity to do any other place. "Circles gives you the opportunity to give back to the project and to other people, where other social service programs don't offer that."

In her Circle, Diane worked on doing some concrete budgeting, which was something she had never learned. "All I learned about money growing up was [that] we never had any. Actually having money and budgeting it was a really big concept." She felt comfortable sharing details of her financial situation. "It was a no-blame, no-shame environment. You say, 'This is where I am . . .' I made decisions that were not all smart ones, but I knew I had to take responsibility for [my situation] if I wanted to make things better."

The other thing Diane did as a result of Circles was clean up her credit report. "I had bills that I couldn't pay when I was going to school, and when I was working a minimum-wage job there were things I couldn't pay that went into collections, and I ran some credit cards up, and so those are things that I paid off." She also entered into an asset-development program in her state that matched everything she put in three to one. "I'm actually buying a house in about two weeks with the money I built up with that. It's exciting!" She also went back to school to finish her degree in sociology, which helped her find a great job.

While Diane was a Circle leader, a position opened up as a Circles coordinator. "I was able to stop my participation and work into this role of being a coach to families and facilitator of our weekly meeting." She now works directly with families in Circles. "I think that there is a moral responsibility to help other people in our community."

Diane grew up thinking that if you work hard you can make it, but she has known so many people who work hard and still can't get ahead. "I think there is something inherently wrong with our economic system—and that we have a responsibility to speak up about it." She has seen firsthand many public policies that keep people trapped in poverty. "I think I have the responsibility to make other people understand that public policy needs to change." She thinks community members need to be more aware of the poverty around them. "If people are in poverty, it affects everyone; and if everybody prospers, it affects everyone. We are all interconnected."

In my community of Story County, Iowa, the truth during 1999 was that families earning $25,000 or less per year comprised more than 8,000 households (CACI Marketing Systems, personal communication). Given the escalating costs of housing, healthcare, childcare, transportation, and food, people earning such meager incomes *cannot* pay for their basic needs. Our economic system does not provide enough livable wage jobs. Our communities do not provide enough affordable housing. Our nation does not provide support for adequate health insurance, putting far too many people in jeopardy. And, along with these systemic issues, individuals bring their own problems to the equation, including:

- Domestic abuse that forces a woman and her children to leave their home
- Not doing well in school, therefore avoiding (or not finishing) college or good vocational training

- Developing an addiction, then lacking access to resources—that is, *people* with sufficient knowledge, care, and skill—to successfully interrupt it
- Having children at a too-early age without adequate support from another adult

Once in poverty, people very rapidly become isolated. They frequently don't have a reliable car, money for gas, or a regularly working phone. They need to move to areas where the rent is lower, which often may be farther away from job opportunities, thereby setting up a no-win situation, further exacerbating their problems. Now they don't feel comfortable attending places of worship in more affluent neighborhoods. The welfare system is invasive and scary: Programs are inflexible, and benefits end too soon, before people are back on their feet. Sometimes jobs may be plentiful, but existing agencies may have a difficult time linking those who need jobs with those who need workers. Clearly, every family situation is unique, which is why uniform solutions offered by large government programs fail so consistently to reduce poverty.

The good news is that all of this is completely solvable. We simply need more people who are willing to commit to doing what's necessary to make sure that all children have enough to eat—that all families can pay the cost of their basic needs and have some left over to invest for the future. We call these individuals *allies.*

If you have plenty to eat—and are willing to work to help everyone have enough to eat—you will grow beyond any words I can use. It's an amazing privilege to help another human being meet basic needs. Once enough of us commit ourselves to this goal, we will truly be on our way to eliminating poverty. From my own experience, I can assure you that denial, rationalization, and judgmentalism fall away as we come to personally know people who are suffering in poverty. Life improves, not just for those we help, but for all of us.

Ben, an ally, believes strongly in the Circles Campaign. "When I was growing up, people had more siblings around—parents, grandparents, and extended family—and I think nowadays people have [fewer] siblings and move around a lot more. I see Circles as a potential for replacing that connection that people used to have." Another benefit of Circles, according to Ben, is that it has been good to cross the socio-economic boundaries that people put up in their lives. "You see over and over again that people don't have many others to count on. A Circle allows them to be with people that [normally] they would not necessarily deal with—and to provide them some positive outlooks in their lives."

Ben sees the potential for Circles growing. "I've been around a while looking at the way things are [done]. I see this as a very logical alternative to what is being offered out there, and a much better alternative." He believes that Circles gives people the chance to change their own lives. "It's more of the 'hands-up' than a 'hand-out' type of thing. We really put the emphasis on the person wanting to make a change in their life and give them a little bit of motivation to get them to the next level."

"I've gotten out of Circles an appreciation of what people experience and the challenges in life." Ben has seen some highly motivated people who are participants and allies. "They have their heart in the right place, and they only want to have success, not only in their own way, but in others'; wanting to share in their time—that's a huge thing nowadays—people willing to share their time to help others."

If you're not already an ally, you can begin by investigating why people living near you are poor and what can be done about it. Reading this book will show you that there's a concrete plan to follow to change both your life and your community in ways that can help to reduce and, eventually, eliminate poverty.

CHAPTER 4

Expand Social Networks: Relate Outside Your 'Comfort Zone'

We all like the idea of having the freedom to pursue our dreams, to pursue quality in life, to pursue comfort and luxury. In the United States, 5% of the population holds more than 20% of the total wealth, while the poorest 40% holds just 12.8%. These figures force us to see that this basic right to pursue happiness is actually not a real possibility for everyone. For numerous reasons, each of us doesn't have an equal opportunity to pursue wealth or even to make informed and free choices about our preferred standard of living. If equal opportunity were a reality, 40% of us wouldn't be working for an income insufficient for providing food, clothing, and acceptable housing—and 15.9% wouldn't be living without health insurance. These are not reasonable *choices.*

Each one of us needs to realize that people having incomes that exceed levels required for comfortable living were not born with some inherent quality rendering them somehow more deserving than those whose incomes are inadequate to meet the basic needs of human survival. In spite of this truth, many of the 60% in our middle- and high-income levels were born with clear-cut advantages, like having access to better education, connections to high-earning social networks, and role models who understand how to make a lot of money.

The reasons for this are numerous and include complex social influences, such as racism and sexism.

Every person is born with a remarkable intelligence that allows processing of a nearly infinite amount of data in order to make appropriate decisions throughout life. The truth is, if we are raised poor, we learn a lot about being poor. If we are raised in the middle-income level, we learn what it takes to stay in the middle. If we are raised in a wealthy home, we learn how the wealthy live. As Dr. Payne has pointed out, when individuals from any income level are suddenly thrust into a significantly different one, learning and applying appropriate coping skills literally can become a matter of survival.

Even when the pervasive barrier of racism is not an overwhelming factor, and no matter what our family's income, eventually we learn to associate with people from similar *economic* backgrounds. As that happens, we tend to keep our distance from people living with a lot more money—or a lot less. We may take on social causes that help "the poor," but rarely will we build a meaningful relationship with someone who has significantly less income. Similarly, as someone with very few assets, we may join a place of worship whose members mostly earn middle-level incomes, but rarely will we try to build deep relationships with those we meet there.

OPPORTUNITIES VARY BASED ON INCOME LEVEL

Because we strive to live in a democracy where ideally all people have an equal chance to succeed economically, we try to develop educational institutions that we hope work equally well for everyone. In reality, they don't. For example, only one in ten children from a household with an annual income of $25,000 or less goes to college. Some say this is because these children and their parents are making bad decisions. Others say there is something about the education system—from pre-school to college—that favors children from homes with more income. A study in Marshalltown, Iowa, showed that children from homes with $10,000 or less annual income were involved in one extracurricular activity per year, while their peers from homes with $40,000 or more in annual income participated in more than six such activities per year. When children increase their competency and confidence by engaging in additional developmental activities, they become more likely to succeed because of the resulting benefits, which accrue over time.

RELATING WITH THOSE HAVING SIGNIFICANTLY DIFFERENT INCOMES IS DIFFICULT

We are taught to build relationships with people earning about the same amount we do. If you are in the poorest fifth of our country's population, where the average annual household income is $9,589, chances are your main relationships are with people who also fall into this quintile. If you earn a middle income, averaging $46,830/year, you probably have friends within that range. And if you were born into a household in the top-fifth income category of $125,000 or more/year—or you have figured out how to get into it—you have probably established relationships primarily with people also earning at this level. In my own life, I have yet to see anyone build a strong, close relationship with someone who is several quintiles of income apart—*unless* it was done with strong intention. This crossover doesn't come naturally.

Becoming intentional about ending poverty means we must get intentional about building in-depth relationships with those having very different income levels. We have to *really* want to change the way we do business in order to ensure that *everyone* has the support, resources, and opportunities necessary to become fully employed and self-sufficient. There is something uncomfortable about establishing more than a polite relationship with someone who has a lot more money, or a lot less money, than we have. Both groups can feel threatened—or at least uneasy. Both can struggle with feelings of guilt and anger. We want the other person to be wrong in some way so that we can continue living our lives, knowing that it's acceptable to keep our distance. The commitment to extend oneself to those who live with much more or much less by caring about their well-being at a new level can result in strong new relationships.

OVERCOMING RACISM

When trying to establish personal relationships with those in other income brackets, understanding racism frequently becomes part of the task. Sadly, our nation was built on policies and practices that continue to serve the interests of European Americans at the expense of Native Americans, African Americans, and people from other ethnic backgrounds.

As a "white" descendant of European Americans, I was born into immediate privilege. Our primary institutions were designed to protect and preserve this privilege, and our culture remains infused with such notions. Because society has given me the advantage, often I can be quick to deny that racism exists, because I just don't experience it. But if I am to relate genuinely with a person whose race is different from mine, I must first honestly confront the fact that in our nation we still struggle on an uneven playing field that is slanted heavily toward "whites." Once I acknowledge this, my denial is reduced, and I can open up internally enough to become a much more effective ally in the often parallel struggles to dismantle racism *and* poverty. I can best learn by listening closely to those who experience racism, allowing them to guide me in ways that will ultimately move all of us beyond these destructive social constructs. Obviously, this subject demands much more attention than can be given here, and I encourage you to pursue it further.

NEW RELATIONSHIPS CAN BE CREATED

The good news is that it *is possible* to establish enjoyable friendships with individuals from all walks of life, to move together beyond racism, and to break through perceived cultural barriers. It takes commitment and a deep-seated desire to succeed. I am learning how to do it myself. Here are some insights:

- I have information that can help my new friends make more income. It's acceptable to share that information with them—if they want it.
- I have social contacts and networks that may prove useful to my new friends in a wide variety of ways.
- I have more money. It's all right to spend it on helping my friends. It's also all right to choose not to spend it. I don't need to worry about anyone else's expectations.
- Sharing is something that can be talked about openly and honestly between friends.

- I don't have to stand by and watch people suffer economically. I can jump in and offer help. I can encourage them to ask for help when they need it.
- I don't have to be perfect. It's OK to make mistakes.
- I can let my friends do whatever they want to do without getting wrapped up in whether they actually take any of my advice or use the resources I offer.
- It's OK to let go of relationships if they are simply too much work and are not fulfilling. I don't have to stick around just because I think I should. In the long run any relationship needs to be enjoyable to both parties.
- There are plenty of wonderful things to do that don't require money. I can open myself up to possibilities for fun in order to include friends who have less money than I do.
- It's *really* OK not to worry about making mistakes. There are very few instructions from society about how to relate to those in different income categories. When I pursue a friendship with someone who earns much more or much less money than I do, I am being a pioneer.

Making these new friends is vital to building a stronger, safer society for all of us. Poverty will end when enough people in our communities decide to do what it takes to end it. I believe that the motivation and energy for this task will come from having real relationships with people who are suffering in poverty. Trying to build these friendships is worth the initial awkwardness. In doing so, we'll begin to think more clearly about problems related to poverty, as well as about potential solutions for them. In addition, and perhaps most importantly, we'll feel less isolated as we step out of the comfort zone of our own economic brackets and into promising new relationships.

PART III

Ending Poverty in Our Time

I grew up in the United States during the '60s and '70s when most people living in the suburbs just assumed things would become better and better. I expected to enjoy a future like that. Moreover, my life as an adult in the work world has been upwardly mobile from day one. I am a "white" male, have a college education, and was raised in a family with two breadwinning professionals. In our culture, the social and economic cards have always been stacked in my favor.

In the U.S. today there are many millions of others—thankfully including men and *women from* all *backgrounds—who have similar economic advantages. As a group of well-off "baby boomers," we have a lot of influence in this country. We vote, we have money, and we have friends in influential positions. Most of us, however, are just as confused as the next person about the causes and effects of poverty.*

When we as a group accept the challenge of focusing more clearly and intentionally on eliminating poverty in this country, we will become formidable allies for the millions of families who face a daily struggle to survive without enough.

CHAPTER 5

Defining 'Poverty'

Before the late 1700s and early 1800s, society's *haves* were kings, queens, rich religious and military figures, some wealthy merchants, and landowners. Everyone else was destitute. Poverty reigned everywhere. It was the human condition. All that changed with the Industrial Revolution. More people obtained jobs, earned money, and even owned land. In the United States, we built a "middle class" with policies like the Homestead Act, the GI Bill, and a variety of grants and loans for education and other kinds of social development. We gave regular folks their piece of land to own and work. With Social Security, we protected millions of elderly people from falling into poverty. So, while there is much controversy about what the real poverty rate in this country is today, given the antiquated formula used to determine these figures (see below), there is clearly much less poverty now than before these public policies were implemented during the 20th century.

According to the U.S. Census Bureau, in this country the poverty rate dropped from 22.4% in 1959 to its lowest level of 11.1% in 1973. It was 12.6% in 2005. Today federal guidelines suggest our poverty rate is still less than 13%. Professionals and other experienced people agree that the real rate is 2 to 3 *times* that figure.

Poverty, in financial terms, is the inability to consistently pay for the basic needs of food, clothing, shelter, healthcare, transportation, and childcare. Federal guidelines were developed in the 1960s. The Census Bureau still determines the rate by taking the cost of food, multiplying it by 3, then assuming that a family living under this figure is "poor." However, increases in the costs of healthcare and housing have grown at much faster rates than the cost of food over the past four decades, rendering this assessment method *totally* obsolete. Unfortunately, we never have had the political will to change the formula in order to more accurately represent the true picture of poverty in our nation.

Poverty undermines democracy by disempowering vast numbers of voters and potential voters, preventing them from having a voice in our government. As long as some people are too busy surviving to pay attention to politics, there will be those who *can and will* wield enormous power over them. Furthermore, the "great middle class" of the 20th century is eroding. Not one of us should be complacent about letting our nation move back toward our autocratic origins, a time when the few ruled over the exhausted and frightened many.

Even if we accept a worst-case estimate of 40% living in poverty in this country, we can see that this means at least 60% of our citizens successfully meet their basic needs on a consistent basis. Will we be able to increase that figure? Will we fall back into even greater poverty? Will it ever be possible to get to a time when there simply will be *no* poverty in this country? Maybe. Pursuing goals to move us in the direction of having a 0% poverty rate will provide us with bolder, more substantial ideas than if we assume that nothing much can (or, worse, should) be done about it. The federal government could and should take major steps to end poverty in the United States. State governments could and should take steps to end poverty, working hand in hand with federal, county, and city governments. Individuals in communities across the nation could and should do much more to alleviate poverty in their midst.

Resources and ideas are already available. Certain strategies have already begun to prove useful. And, challenging the "more-for-me-is-better" mindset in our culture (which, quite ironically, has normalized poverty) is one of the most important things anyone can do to help bring about change.

CHAPTER 6

Housing and the Elimination of Poverty

The task of eliminating poverty begins with each one of us. The more we discuss poverty to understand its causes, the better we become at responding to it effectively. Poverty is established and sustained in a community by a number of elements, including:

- Escalating costs of housing, healthcare, and childcare
- Children having children
- Parents separating
- Low-wage jobs
- Lack of universal medical insurance
- High cost of transportation
- A fragmented "safety net"

We can each use our unique talents and resources to start clearing away problems that stand in the way of eliminating poverty. Housing is a good place to begin.

The cost of housing is often the largest expense in a family's budget. Let's say a person earns $36,000/year and has one preschooler who needs childcare (because he or she is working). After taxes are deducted, paying for the costs of childcare, fuel and car insurance to get to and from work, special clothes that wouldn't be needed except for the job, and other work-related expenses, this person may be left with a net income of only $7.50/hour. (I encourage you to do this exercise for your own situation: It's a very interesting, enlightening experience.) Now, if there are mortgage payments on a $100,000 loan, an 8% interest rate will consume $4 of the $7.50. Add principal, property tax, utilities, homeowner's insurance, and probably a primary mortgage insurance (PMI) fee for not making a down payment of 20%, and it's now likely that $6 of the $7.50 has been spent. There will be a tax break of about $1 at the end of year, so expenses for housing are $5 of the net $7.50. This means that *two out of every three hours* on the job go toward putting a roof over this worker's head!

I wish I could say that paying rent is a better scenario, but that's not the case. In fact, it's often worse because, in contrast to mortgage payments, there's no tax break for rent payments, nor does capital accumulate for future use. This is why obtaining affordable housing is such a crucial milestone on the journey out of poverty. Given current housing costs, our goal needs to be helping people find jobs that pay at least $10/hour *with health benefits.* That is fully 25% more than the typical wage currently found by people leaving welfare. Just imagine what housing expenses look like to someone earning $10/hour or less. The "typical" family leaving welfare is a mother and two young children. At $10/hour, that's only $20,000/year—with *two* children in childcare. It's a financial nightmare.

The housing crisis can be solved with a steady focus on the following major strategies:

- New housing opportunities need to be developed for families having annual incomes of less than $30,000. To begin to address this problem, the communities of Story County, Iowa—including the city of Ames—formed a partnership to leverage federal dollars that can buy down the cost of a new home for people with modest incomes. This effort needs all the support it can get from the public. A housing assessment study conducted in 1998 determined that in the ensuing 10 years, Story County's needs would include 832 new units renting for under $400/month, 728 rental units in the $400–$500/month range, 501 new homes to sell in the $60,000–$80,000 range, and 606 homes selling for $80,000–$110,000. Similar situations certainly exist across the nation.

  Without a significant investment by the federal government, local communities do not have the capacity to develop affordable-housing needs identified in assessment studies like these. We, the public, need to let our federal representatives know that housing must be a top priority during the coming decade. Affordable housing has been identified for years by one community needs assessment after another as one of our most pressing problems. We'll all share in the benefits of living near citizens enjoying stable and affordable housing. But this won't happen without grassroots leadership to inspire federal policies that support reinvesting in our nation's housing stock, so that it once again becomes affordable for hard-working individuals earning modest wages to own their homes.

- Another step taken in Story County was the establishment of a community land trust. Simply stated, the idea is to put land into a trust held by a nonprofit organization, and then lease it to a homebuyer for $1/year. The trust stipulates that the resale value of the home on this land will always be kept at an affordable level. This is one way to ensure that a community investment in housing stays in the community. Homebuyers earn capital as time progresses, but policies prevent them from making quick returns on the community's investment. The land's value is removed from the cost to the buyer, which makes housing far more affordable. Land trusts accept donated and/or discounted land, as well as cash contributions to help purchase land.

- Habitat for Humanity is very strong in Story County. This organization is building twice as many homes there as it averages for the nation. Habitat is a great program that can add a few new low-cost homes to a community every year. You can help by volunteering and/or donating money to the organization.

- There are extensive expenses associated with "upgrading" one's living quarters. For example, Realtor and bank fees are paid every time a house changes ownership, with the cumulative effect of driving up the cost of the home for subsequent buyers.

Our banker told me that we had stayed in our Marshalltown home two and half years longer than the average Iowan stays in a home—which is only for four years. Do we need to upgrade so often? Are we ready to work the additional hours required to live in our new home? Is that what we really want? Or are there other ways to fulfill our needs that won't have such a profound impact on our personal expenses and, over time, increase the overall cost of housing in our community?

- Building codes, which are there to protect us all, come at a price. Are they all necessary? Can we reform these codes to lessen the cost of building a house? For example, the cost of adhering to strict historical-preservation codes can severely impact efforts to repair old houses. Other restrictions that can limit the number of affordable-housing units in the community are ones like those that prohibit the addition of a "granny flat" onto an existing home.

- Good community design concepts can drive *down* the price of housing. Plans combining higher density and manufactured housing with attractive green space, minimal street setbacks, alleys behind homes, and narrow streets can dramatically decrease construction costs and at the same time provide opportunities for increased social interaction.

- Finally, consider this notion: An increase in the sale price of an individual home drives up the cost of every other home in that community. The Ames area has aging and deteriorating housing stock, so the demand for new stock has increased. This demand has, in turn, raised the expectations of developers, bankers, insurance companies, Realtors, landowners, home sellers, attorneys, and everyone else who receives a percentage of the total sale price. How much square footage is enough to be happy? In 1949 the median size of a new home in the United States was

> 1,100 square feet. In 1970 it was 1,385. In 1993 it was 2,060, and in 2005 the National Association of Home Builders announced it had reached an all-time high of 2,434 square feet. If we consider how many additional work hours we're exchanging for our bigger home, is owning more square footage, with all the attendant extra costs, a rational choice? We aren't likely to be encouraged by any of the groups mentioned above to be modest with our choices. So, let this be one voice in support of taking a long and hard look at the actual returns on upgrading.

Each of us has our own reference group on whom we draw—our family, friends, associates—to determine what and how much to consume in life. It's all too easy to let our reference group shape the majority of our purchasing choices. In fact, it's very difficult to do otherwise. This is one of many reasons to intentionally develop relationships with those earning significantly more *and* less than we do.

There are many good alternatives to joining the "suburban sprawl" movement. Our nation is full of people who have chosen to simplify their lives by scaling back on the square footage they need to feel fulfilled; they're consuming less and working fewer hours in order to enjoy life more. I encourage you to add at least one of these folks to your primary reference group.

To live in poverty-free communities that aren't just exclusive enclaves for those who have large financial resources is a vision worth pursuing in the United States. We have enough goodwill and intelligence in our nation to solve this puzzle. The problem of high housing costs must be addressed in a powerful way in order to free us all from the tremendous burden it imposes.

CHAPTER 7

Supporting Families

The elimination of poverty requires that, among many other things, communities respond more adequately to crises occurring when couples with children separate. This response can't be left entirely to private and public agencies—or even to religious organizations. We need to take more individual responsibility for helping our friends and families.

For some parents losing a job is so devastating that they literally run away from the family. This almost always compounds any existing problems and creates new ones. Sometimes drug and alcohol abuse is involved. As neighbors, friends, or relatives, we can often make a difference by genuinely caring and offering our support in whatever ways possible to help struggling parents address their problems head-on.

If parents won't seek out help for themselves, we as friends and family can learn how to change our own responses so that at least we're not enabling destructive behavior. This requires being honest and direct—and keeping the well-being of any children present in mind throughout the course of our conversations. Sometimes it can be helpful to seek advice from a trained counselor about how to offer empowering, rather than enabling, support.

According to a source with the Iowa Department of Human Services, approximately five out of six families on welfare in Story County consist of single mothers with children (personal communication). Although things in this country may be changing somewhat, historically most families who go into poverty do so when the father is not providing financially for his family. From my work with people leaving welfare I've learned that men who abandon their responsibilities need a number of supports if they're going to become functional dads.

One important reason that men who struggle with being a parent do so is because so often they lack sufficient social support. Men, in general, tend to be more isolated than women. This lack of engagement with others clearly can contribute to having difficulty with the responsibilities of caring for children. Each of us can help by simply talking to the men in our lives about whether they have people to turn to when the going gets rough.

If a man has abused his partner and/or children, he needs encouragement from friends and family to be able to admit his behavior and get whatever help he needs to stop it. He also will need to make amends and, once he becomes stable enough for it, to re-engage with his family in whatever ways work for all parties, if that door is opened to him again. He may have done such serious damage, though, that the best outcome he can hope for is to support his family financially from a distance.

Nevertheless, a frequent situation encountered by families in poverty is that of a man not paying child support. When this is the case, once again he must first admit his behavior and then find a way to meet his financial obligations to his children. Taking these steps often requires tremendous support from friends and family.

When abuse is present in a family, everyone involved needs to act at once to end it. Women who are being victimized by abuse must get support immediately. Much less frequently, men can become victims of abusive partners. This is not a very widely acknowledged problem, but it does happen. Men in these kinds of relationships are often reluctant to seek help from friends and family to sort out how to handle the situation, but they desperately need this support. Abused and abusive partners and their children may all benefit from professional counseling to learn more about how to cope.

So, of course, women must share responsibility for families falling apart. Women who continually enter into relationships with irresponsible men and bear their children also need the gift of honest conversation from those close to them. To not bring up concerns about this dangerous behavior is to not care enough. Each of us has an obligation to tell the truth in ways that might help break these cycles. It's not easy, to be sure, but it must be done—and done lovingly and compassionately in the context of a relationship.

Regardless of the reason that a couple doesn't stay together to raise their children, in our society it is women who are almost always left carrying the responsibility. For me, the appropriate response to this situation is providing care and compassion to all involved. Who knows what might happen if we learn how to talk about our concerns without evoking judgments that push away those we love? Effective communication that results in deeper understanding can lead to wonderful changes in the lives of family members. Ultimately, this is the sort of support everyone can learn to do better in order to help eliminate the terrible condition of poverty from our communities.

CHAPTER 8

Childcare Assistance

In order to become financially self-sufficient, people need access to dependable, affordable childcare. The state must provide assistance for this in order for welfare reform to work. Let me illustrate how important childcare assistance is for just one family in Story County who has experienced many problems commonly encountered by those living in poverty.

> Sarah left her husband after he abused her for the last time. Her life is not at all what she imagined it would be when she started her family; she never thought she'd have to take care of an infant and a 4-year-old by herself. She doesn't expect to receive any child support for a long time, if ever. She left welfare by taking the first job offered to her because that is what state policy dictated she must do. She is now working for a local company earning $7.30/hour, which is the average starting wage for people just getting off welfare in Story County.
>
> Sarah needs a car to go to work and received a donated one from our program. She receives childcare assistance from the state. She doesn't have subsidized rent and therefore pays $500/month, plus $150/month for utilities. Her new paycheck is $950/month when she gets full-time hours. After rent and utilities, she has $300/month to pay for gasoline, car repairs, car insurance, food, clothes, diapers, other necessities, and emergencies!

If Sarah can figure out how to leave this $7.30/hour job for one that pays at least $10/hour, or about $1,700/month, we would say she has a good chance of leaving welfare permanently. That is, of course, if she continues to receive childcare assistance.

If Sarah loses her childcare assistance, she will pay $570/month for infant care and about $500/month for her 4-year-old. Obviously, in this situation a paycheck of $950/month—or even $1,700/month—won't cover her expenses. She'll have to go back on welfare until her children can attend school. That is not what Sarah wants to do.

We need to make providing help for quality childcare a very high priority. What is good for children and parents is ultimately good for everyone. Creating stability now for families engaged in the working world will give rise to a healthier population in 20 years, when today's children are adults.

PART IV

Be a Bolder Ally

Mahatma Gandhi said we must be *the change we want to see. If we claim our role in helping to make our communities—and the systems that serve them—better, we will inspire transformation that can* dismantle *poverty. Highly detailed plans are not necessary before initiating efforts that will make a difference to others.*

Becoming *the change you want to see happen causes a disturbance in the status quo. What each of us needs to do in order to fulfill our particular part will become clearer by simply taking the next logical step.*

If we are to ensure that everyone in our community has enough money, meaning, and friendship to thrive, we must also be willing to turn our attention to our own lives and make necessary changes. This section is devoted to inspiring and equipping you to live a life that contributes to achieving a better, thriving society in which poverty is nonexistent.

CHAPTER 9

Eliminate Clutter to Focus Energy on Building Community

Earlier in my life there were many times when it seemed to me that I was drowning in *stuff.* It was hard to wake up and see the world as it really was when I was buried under an avalanche of papers, unfinished projects, and a chaotic environment of *things.* Some say they thrive in this kind of "creative mess." I think most people do not. Getting one's home in order can be seen as a spiritual practice, one that frees energy for living in ways that are more connected to inner directives, which will ultimately enhance the well-being of the entire community.

Clutter can be defined as anything in life that no longer serves a useful purpose. For example, the box of recipes we never use is clutter. The children's clothes and special drawings that are stashed in boxes in the closet, garage, attic, and basement are potentially clutter—if we've saved so many that we aren't enjoying them anymore. A relationship with someone who takes energy from us each and every time we interact is clutter. Junk foods, junk activities, and just plain junk create clutter inside our bodies and inside our lives. The more clutter we allow, the less likely we are to notice and embrace things of value.

I have been in homes where the carpeting has disappeared under toy pieces. Little itty-bitty plastic knobs, buttons, doll parts, and cardboard paper parts stretch from wall to wall. Lots of "stuff"—little meaning. In our culture, we risk teaching our children from early on that life is mostly about forming a relationship with *stuff.*

Clearing away clutter frees us from the headaches caused by keeping all of it around. Having too much "stuff" steals our time and attention, threatening to leave us with lives that are short on meaning. Finding *meaning*, not accumulating material possessions, is the real source of fulfillment. Getting rid of clutter allows room for meaning to find its way more deeply into our lives. Getting rid of clutter means never again having to waste time cleaning it, organizing it, or otherwise attending to it.

Fulfillment is the result of pursuing purposeful activity. Fulfillment derives from activities that bring enjoyment, don't hurt others, and don't hurt the planet. Any activity that betrays any of these criteria will prove less fulfilling.

When we let clutter sit around in our homes and vehicles, we tend to clutter our daily agenda with activities that are largely a waste of our time. These are activities we don't enjoy doing, but which we feel compelled to do for various reasons. We meet with people who drain us, but we feel obligated to continue interacting with them. We engage in activities that we know harm other people, but we rationalize and stop paying attention to what we're doing. We consume products knowing they've been produced using processes that pollute the earth, but we buy them anyway. All of our decisions, conscious or unconscious, to continue these activities can ultimately diminish our sense of fulfillment. They're an important form of *clutter*.

Having jobs we don't like in order to fill up big houses with *stuff* we don't really need or want in order to fill the hole created by a lack of meaningful work is a vicious cycle in which many seem to feel trapped. Better to live in less expensive housing and do what we find really satisfying than to settle for a job that ends up compromising our core values.

We need to pursue purposeful activity so much more than we need to buy *things*. Life is too valuable to waste. The earth is too valuable to abuse. We need to trust that life ultimately will support a choice to pursue meaningful activity.

On my deathbed, will I be thinking, "I'm pleased with how I've enjoyed sharing my life with others" or "I wish I could have filled up the family room with more *stuff*"?

We don't need to let clutter control us. Get rid of clutter to free up psychic energy for pursuing life's work. Hire a personal organizer to help get your home so fine-tuned that it becomes a pleasure to step into each room. This investment can easily pay for itself in savings from better purchasing decisions in the future. Hello, Salvation Army, community garage sale, and the local recycling center! It's time to *declutter.*

CHAPTER 10

The Concept of Enough

How Lifestyle Choices, the Environment, and Poverty Are Interrelated

Our relationship to poverty is connected to our relationship with our natural environment. We human beings, particularly in the United States, sometimes seem to be behaving like children with a bagful of candy, eating up resources until we get sick.

North Americans are extremely productive. By many measures we have succeeded, beyond the wildest dreams of previous generations. Our wealth, however, has come with personal, social, and environmental price tags. Consider, for example, these statistics about the U.S. compiled in the early '90s by the New Road Map Foundation:

- Parents spent 40% less time with their children than they did in 1965.
- Employees spent 163 hours more per year on the job than they did in 1969.
- Teenagers were exposed to 360,000 advertisements by the time they graduated from high school.
- Adults spent six *hours* a week shopping, 40 *minutes* a week playing with their children.
- The waste we generated each year in the United States at that time would have filled a convoy of 10-ton garbage trucks 145,000 miles long—more than half-way to the moon.

If anything, things since then have only gotten worse.

Revealing insight about whether or not we're enjoying our affluence comes from a 1988 poll of people in the United States, which showed that the feeling of "not yet enough" persists as income rises. When asked if they had achieved "the American Dream," not surprisingly only 5% of those earning less than $15,000/year said yes, but quite surprisingly only 6% of those earning more than $50,000/year said yes. At the same time, more than 69% of the population reported that they would like to "slow down and live a more relaxed life."

OUR ENVIRONMENT

Our relatively new affluence exacts a global price.

- A person in the United States causes 100 times more damage to the global environment than a person in a poor country. Hard to imagine? Among all humans, 8% own a car: Among households in the U.S., 89% own one or more cars. In this country 250 gallons of oil are consumed *per person* (including children and others who don't drive) per year, twice the figure for Europe.
- A European produces less than half the waste of a citizen of the United States.
- In the last 200 years, the U.S. has lost 50% of its wetlands, 90% of its northwestern old-growth forests, and 99% of its tall-grass prairie.
- One-fifth of the groundwater pumped annually in the U.S. is not renewable.
- We turn over 9 square miles of rural land to development every day.
- We lose 1 million acres of cropland to erosion every year.
- In the U.S. 186 quarts of soft drinks (but only 149 quarts of water) are consumed per capita per year. The total energy required to produce one 12-ounce can of diet soda is 2,200 calories (compared to the 1 calorie we gain from drinking it).

The mainstream news media are finally beginning to report accurately on the long-standing consensus in the international scientific community concerning evidence that human activity *does* contribute to climate change, and on the growing sense of urgency among scientists regarding the need to address global warming. We in this nation at last appear poised to face our environmentally abusive consumption habits. Each person living in this country has an immediate responsibility to work to drastically reduce the collective high-carbon diet of the U.S. According to Environmental Defense, our most significant energy use occurs in four primary sectors: homes (and other buildings), private cars, industry, and agriculture. Every individual can make a critical difference by making lifestyles adjustments that will serve to guard our environment for the benefit of future generations. We need to demonstrate a willingness to change, and we need to require that our government leads the way in this crucial endeavor, thereby setting an example for the rest of the nations on our planet.

OUR LIFESTYLES

Many in the United States are beginning to question the common assumption that more is always better. As we've seen, the high cost of housing, the most tangible source of misery for the poorest third of our society, is driven by the "more-is-better" mentality. The median size of a single-family home nearly doubled between 1949 and 1993. Now it's virtually impossible to buy a new house for less than $100,000 in any community in North America. In the U.S., more than 10 million people maintain two or more homes, yet only half of the total population owns the house they live in. The other half competes in a rental market of scarce older housing stock, since older homes tend to be torn down or turned into more expensive units. Many people in poverty or close to it spend *more than half* of their paychecks to put a roof over their heads!

The marketing experts in our society call out to "Buy now, pay later." Americans are feeling the pressure of increasingly materialistic expectations. Here are some results of a November 2005 holiday poll of 500 American adults conducted for the Center for a New American Dream:

- The high cost of living is the #1 concern of Americans as they approach the holiday season.
- More worry about the high cost of living (53%) and their personal financial situation (50%) than about economic insecurity (40%) or the war in Iraq (37%).
- Nearly all polled (91%) say the cost of living has increased compared to last year, and more than 2 out of 3 blame the price of oil or gas (68%).
- Nearly 3 out of 5 (59%) say they incur credit card debt during the holiday season.
- Nearly one-third (32%) say it took them more than three months to pay off this credit card debt last year; 14% said they were still paying it off as the next holiday season approached.
- More than 3 out of 4 (78%) wish that holidays were less materialistic.
- Nearly 9 out of 10 (87%) believe that holidays should be more about family and caring for others, not giving and receiving gifts.
- More than 3 out of 4 (76%) say that kids are too materialistic and the holiday season just makes things worse.
- Nearly 4 out of 5 of these Americans polled (79%) *do not* believe that it's necessary to spend a lot of money in order to have a fulfilling and enjoyable holiday; many say they want to give gifts this year that encourage savings.

The amount of income put into savings dropped from 8.6% in 1973 to 4.2% in 1993. In 2005, the national savings rate had dipped below 0%. According to Newsweek, as of August, 2006 Americans for the first time owed more money than they made in a year. Consumer debt was at a record $2.17 trillion and we cashed out an amazing $431 billion in home equity in 2005.

YOUR MONEY OR YOUR LIFE

People are feeling the pain of pursuing lifestyles that are well past the "enough" mark. What is enough? Enough is a highly personal figure. One of the best ways to arrive at it is to monitor expenses for several months in a row. In the book *Your Money or Your Life*, Joe Dominguez and Vicki Robin outline a nine-step procedure for reducing personal expenses to reach one's own sustainable level of "enough." People following the steps put aside money regularly until they have sufficient capital to generate enough interest income to cover monthly expenses. The authors suggest tracking decreasing expenses and increasing interest income each month. At the "cross-over" point where these match, financial independence is achieved. After this time, within the limits of interest income, any lifestyle or agenda can be pursued without the *need* to work for a steady paycheck.

When we modify our *overworking-to-pay-for-lots-of-stuff* lifestyles, we free up more time and energy to be allies to families in poverty.

NO PLACE LIKE HOME

Where we choose to live greatly impacts our personal "enough" income level. Currently, my wife and I can walk to the grocery store, the video store, and the library. We can walk to our church, to the natural foods store, a grocery store, the gym, restaurants, and the locally-owned bookstore. We only need one car. I can walk to my office, the hospital, and the post office. Our mortgage is only one-third of what we could expect to pay in some places. While contemplating moving to another much more expensive neighborhood, I learned to see my community and its virtues in a different light. Life at home *can* hold *enough* to be happy.

DECIDE TO HAVE ENOUGH

The globally pervasive condition of poverty, the result of a huge imbalance in the distribution of wealth worldwide, can almost always be found among the root causes of war and terrorism. Currently we in the United States, who consume a vastly disproportionate share of the world's resources, have become major targets for acts of aggression. Terrorism can be seen as a consequence of not understanding the concept of *having enough*. The majority of humanity still lives in relative poverty. Whether or not (from our perspective) the desperation, greed, jealousy, or rage leading to violent acts is warranted, we live with the reality that terrorism poses a serious threat. Our habitual levels of overconsumption fuel a desire in others to have more.

To achieve the goals of ending poverty and restoring our environment, desirable even for selfish reasons, it is imperative that we align our consumption patterns with what is in the best interest of all of humanity and the planet at large. It will take grassroots and political leadership to move us out of our comfort zones. As far as we can determine, there is only one planet that can support life as we know it. We have to respect what is going on around us: We can no longer afford to remain an insular, isolated society. Many of us in the U.S. are in the luxurious position of having enough resources, education, and insight to take significant positive action to achieve such goals. Using a strong moral compass as a guide, we can work to adjust our consumption patterns, until we take only our rightful share from the global table.

Ending poverty will come about when a critical number of us find our individual levels of *having enough*. Transformational leaders with anti-poverty goals will serve their communities well by connecting the important dots between the concept of *having enough* and the end result of reduced poverty. An over-indulgent lifestyle creates imbalances that hurt the individual, other people, and our planet. Such imbalances create feedback cycles of ever-escalating damage to others and the environment. We can only hope that enough of us recognize these patterns in time to develop adequate mechanisms to rebalance before our systems—social and biological—collapse beyond repair.

Contributing to eliminating poverty means to follow Gandhi's advice to "live simply so that others might simply live."

PART V

Personal Stories

In this section I will allow a few personal stories to address the question of how Circles make a difference more eloquently than I ever could in my own words.

CHAPTER 11

Circle Allies

INTERVIEW WITH ANNA

Anna joined a Circle as an ally because she liked the idea of helping others, especially disadvantaged people. She witnessed discrimination against those living in poverty, and she knows that it's hard to change people's attitudes. "Society tends to form one mindset toward certain individuals, and once that stereotype is set, people are stuck with it, because it's really hard to change people's mentality."

Anna has been an ally in a Circle for about a year, and it has been a huge learning process. "It's really easy to decide when you're on the outside of someone's life to see things that you think the other person needs to do to change. The real lesson for me to learn was that those aren't necessarily the things that she wants to do." Her Circle is just figuring out that the leader doesn't always have the confidence to stand up and say that the goals the group is setting are not things that interest her. This has been a little frustrating sometimes. "We're getting to know each other and getting to understand what she has for goals and what she has for ideas." So far, the focus of the group centers on forming a friendship and establishing trust and support in her life. "It's really hard not to put personal goals on the leader."

Since becoming an ally, Anna has been learning about how people's priorities differ. "It's easy to see that if someone doesn't have a home or food, that should be priority number one, but some of the things I think should be high priorities, others put further down the list, and that is a challenge to accept." Because she has become a friend to her leader, she sees that there are many reasons for these differences.

"Everything that has happened to our participant prior to us becoming involved with her [helped] shape . . . her priorities."

Anna has witnessed many coming into Circles with unhealthy dependencies. "When some people first come in, they don't seem to know how to have or be a friend." She sees them fall into either a "using" role, where they use people instead of befriend them—or a role in which they don't think they're worth the help and support people want to give them. In both cases, Anna believes that the leaders tend to have bad self-images—and that it takes a long time to establish boundaries and confidence in the relationships before they can be in a healthy place to make changes.

Anna's advice to anyone becoming an ally is to have patience. "Don't expect to move mountains. Expect to move a tiny speck of sand, and be happy with that, because that is progress." She has seen too many people come in thinking they'll *fix* a person, then move on to the next person, like an assembly line. "Don't look at it as a [problem] that needs to be fixed. They have to make the fix: You can just help them and be with them as they do it."

INTERVIEW WITH JESSICA

Jessica is a dynamic woman who puts energy into everything she does. She became interested in Circles because it was one of the only programs she had heard of that sounded like it could really make a difference in poverty. "I thought it would be exciting to build a relationship with a family and to be a part of helping them get out of poverty." Jessica was active in getting a Circle started in her town and has been an ally for a family for about a year. She has gained a lot from the experience.

"I have learned so much from this. I thought I was pretty knowledgeable on many subjects, but I learned that I don't know anything about poverty." Jessica has now seen firsthand what people have to deal with in their lives and doesn't know how those families cope with their situations. "It isn't anything like I've experienced. I did not grow up in a wealthy family, but I grew up in a family that knew how to budget and knew how to make ends meet." She has found that now she has much greater empathy for people in different situations.

Jessica also has learned a huge lesson about not judging the choices people make. "Many of the decisions people make are out of necessity, and not knowing any better decision *to* make." She experienced an unforgettable example of this when a Circle leader asked where to buy a cake for her son's birthday. Jessica told her, "I've never bought a birthday cake for the kids; I always thought it was fun to make it at home and have them help me." The woman then told Jessica that her oven didn't work. This was a revelation for Jessica. "No wonder she wanted to buy a birthday cake. I thought it would be a waste of money to buy a cake when she could spend a few dollars to buy a mix, but she didn't have any other option."

Jessica learned a lot from this interaction, and now she uses the story when people around her complain about the choices they see people making. "There are some who think people shouldn't buy convenience food with their food stamps—and I've made those same comments in the past—but now I know that maybe this choice makes sense for this family. It's not a good choice, but they probably don't have another choice."

Another area of change and growth that Jessica has undergone in Circles has been as a result of being an ally. "It's hard to not want to 'fix it' for the family. I don't want anybody fixing me, even though I might need it, so it isn't my place." She has seen with her family that it's hard to get from crisis mode to any other place. "One person in our Circle is always trying to get a budget in place, and I don't think that a budget is where [the leader is right now]. I think survival and how to get from August to September is a hard enough challenge without even thinking about a budget." The leader of Jessica's Circle is at a point where she needs to set goals and dreams for the next year. "Maybe that dream would be easier for her than the day-to-day budgeting. If you have a dream and a goal, maybe you can understand the steps that are going to have to happen to get [there]."

One thing Jessica really emphasized is that becoming an ally is a big commitment. "I don't feel like I've assumed responsibility for the family, but I feel like I've assumed some caring and concern, and it can be a time and emotional drain." She pointed out that it's worth the time and energy, but people need to be aware that the families they will be working with need some care. "I think you have to be willing to be an ally for the long haul, not just to try it for six months and, if it doesn't work, throw in the towel, because I don't think these families need to be thrown away one more time."

CHAPTER 12

Circle Leaders

FIRST TRUST, THEN REAL CHANGES

Jon and his wife, Cynthia, found out about Circles two years ago from their daughter's Head Start program. "We were having trouble keeping propane in our system for heat, and we asked for help; the counselor there told us about Circles." Jon and his wife thought Circles sounded like it was a good idea and signed up to join.

Their family found a lot of support and help through Circles. "It helped to establish us into a community, and we made some friends." Through Circles, Jon felt as if he had a better sense of being—of self-worth. "I found work through one of my allies because he's established in the community and, through friendship with his friends, I was able to find a job." Jon and his wife have an educational ally in their Circle to help with their two daughters. "She is really interested in our children's education. She's a teacher and is really dedicated to wanting to help us and getting our daughter to where she should be." One of their daughters is having problems in school, and their ally helps the family by giving suggestions and ideas about how to get her the best education possible.

One thing Jon knows is that Circles cannot fix your problems for you. "You have to get to know each other first, just basically try to establish a friendship." According to Jon, his group established trust before the real changes could take place. "I wouldn't just listen to their advice if I didn't know them, or tell them everything about my life right away." Now Jon trusts in his allies because they believe in the program, and they see that it works for people. He knows they believe in him as well.

There are still areas that the Circle needs to improve. "We are still working on it. Our Circle doesn't meet as often as we should." One goal that did not work was when Jon and Cynthia first tried to "establish themselves" in the community. "It turned out that this goal wasn't really what we wanted at the time. Since that didn't work, we're a little more into setting solid goals that will work out better for us." Jon feels like it doesn't hurt to try things, that it's all a learning experience. He has found this to be easier to do with the support from his Circle. "It is nice to have more friends and people you're concerned about. Things seem to take care of themselves when you get into the group and stick with it."

Jon plans to be in Circles for a while. "It's a process. You can't just get out of poverty overnight." He has seen other Circles that have failed. "Some people don't want to get out of their comfort zone." Jon thinks that with a little trust, however, there could be great changes for most people. "It helps establish you in the community and gives you a lot more choices." His Circles Campaign also has a vehicle program. "Some people think they're just going to get in [a Circle] and get a car, but it's not about that. It's about getting out of poverty, and if you're committed to the program, then that's when they'll help you out if you need a vehicle for work." Jon has learned that it isn't about going into Circles looking for what they will give you, it's about what you can give yourself. "It's not a quick fix; it's about getting in there and setting goals towards whatever it takes to have a better life."

FINDING A HAND-UP, NOT A HAND-OUT

Rachel is a 41-year-old single mother of three children, ages 8 to 11. The family currently lives in a small town in a southern state. They have been members of a Circle for a year and a half. Rachel and her children's father separated about four years ago, and because of this, their lives changed drastically. "When we were together, we were living paycheck to paycheck. We didn't have to worry too much about where things came from. There would be times where it would be tough, but we weren't real worried."

After he left, Rachel wasn't working outside the home. "All of a sudden, our family went from one income to no income." She did receive child support, but that didn't come close to covering all of the expenses.

It took Rachel nine months to find a job. "There aren't a lot of jobs around. There are some that are easier to get, like McDonald's, but I had to figure out what would be best—because if I got a job at McDonald's, the children lost their Medicaid, and we would lose our food stamps." Rachel was very careful about finding a job that would help with insurance. "My son and I both have severe asthma, so there's usually several doctors' visits for that each winter, and my 10-year-old is pretty accident prone." Eventually, Rachel found a job that had full-time pay with benefits, but she still struggled with her insurance. "When they took the insurance benefits, they took the premiums out of my paycheck, and these were so expensive that I could cover myself, but there was no way that I could pay insurance for my family." Her daughter was supposed to have her tonsils out two years ago, but because she has been on and off Medicaid, she hasn't been able to get the surgery.

Not only was the split hard because of financial reasons, it was emotionally devastating as well. "I've had problems since I was a teenager with depression." Things got really bad at home. "I found it really hard to get out of bed in the morning. I was depressed because I couldn't find a job and didn't know how I was going to provide for the children. I couldn't pay the bills. It got to the point where I wouldn't answer the door or I wouldn't answer the phone or open the mail because, you know, if you don't open the mail the bill doesn't exist. If it doesn't exist, you don't have to worry about paying it. We went through a lot with the utilities shut off."

Rachel didn't start dealing with her depression until about a year after the children's father left. "I was a great actress. If I had to go up to my children's school for something, everybody thought that I was 'super mom.' I should have been in Hollywood: I was a pretty darn good actress. Nobody would've guessed that I had a bad problem with depression and that the power was off at home."

She ended up putting her children into counseling because they had a hard time when their dad moved out. "One day the counselor said, 'Rachel, you know, I think that you need to see the counselor too. You're taking care of your children, but you're not taking care of yourself.' So, I started to go see her." This counselor was the person who introduced Rachel to the Circles Campaign. "I always had trouble asking for any kind of help, but things were really bad at the time." Rachel and her children were living in a house with no power; they were using candles at night. Somebody found out and called Family Services, who threatened to take away her children. "My children had moved out and were living with my mother. I went ahead, I don't know what made me do it, but I called the number for Circles." Rachel learned a little bit about the group and scheduled a meeting. "The first meeting I went to was the first Thursday of July in 2005. I knew from that night, that first meeting, that Circles was something very important—I knew it was going to be something very important in our lives."

"I appreciated that Circles is not a hand-out program, it's a hand-up program." Rachel discovered that her Circle members don't just give her things. "They are very educational. Each participant is paired up with allies. We each have a financial ally, a relationship ally, and an educational ally. Now I don't even refer to them as friends, I refer to them as my family." Rachel has people she can call night or day. "They would pick up the phone and ask what it was that I need. It's a huge family now. You can't rely on one person all the time."

Even after joining Circles, things continued to get worse in Rachel's life. "We lost our house. It was a rent-to-own kind of thing. I couldn't get up because I was so depressed. I couldn't do laundry, I couldn't do dishes, I couldn't cook. Things got really bad." Her kids continued to live with her mom while she was living with different friends who would help her. "The children continued in school and wherever I stayed, I'd get up and go and get them ready for school at my mom's." In the meantime, Rachel was learning things from Circles. "I learned how to handle things, how to take responsibility, how to become involved in my community, and where to go in my community for resources." Through Circles, she got involved with a housing program for the homeless.

In March 2006 Rachel and her children got a home. "It took a little while to get things in order, but then we got the kids moved back over there, and we have been there ever since." Not all has been perfect for the family, but things have changed in many ways. "I went for four months without a job this past fall, but before, when there was something bad that happened, if I had lost a job or couldn't pay an energy bill or something, it was devastating. That turned the depression worse and worse, and there was no light at the end of the tunnel." Rachel is able to take care of herself now. "I have doctors that I go see. I keep my medication under control. I know what I'll go back to if I don't make a good choice and I don't want to go back there."

Now Rachel can see that no matter what, there is always a light at the end of the tunnel. "I knew everything was going to be OK because I've learned a lot through Circles. I didn't expect them to go out and find a job for me, but I knew how to use the resources that I had learned about to go about finding another one." Rachel's family is not out of poverty yet, but that doesn't worry her. "My job's not a high-paying job or anything, but I know that we will be all right with the things I have learned. They are things that I will continue to use."

One area in which Rachel's life has improved immensely is her involvement with the community. "I love talking about Circles. I talk to everybody I can about it. I've spoken at our poverty walk rally. I have spoken in front of our congressman. I've talked to different groups of people at immersion trainings for Circles. I am going to Legislative Day to talk to the legislators about [the huge problem of] getting a job and [then immediately] losing your food stamps and Medicaid . . ."

Rachel is trying to make a difference in how people are treated and how the community looks at people in poverty. "I grew up in an 'upper-middle-class' family. I knew there were poor people out there, but I didn't know why they were poor or where they were at. It was just not something that I really worried about because I didn't know anything about it. Which is true about a lot of people. They don't understand it because they don't know about it. There is the misconception that people are in poverty because they want to be. There was never a day when I was growing up that I said, 'Hey, when I grow up, I want to be in poverty.' I don't. It's not fun."

Rachel believes that being in poverty and being involved in Circles has just made her a stronger person. "It's working with my children too. My children see us doing reciprocity and giving back to our communities, and they're wanting to get involved in doing reciprocity. It's good because it helps the children to understand that they can become part of the community too." Rachel's children are learning that helping others isn't just for grownups.

In her Circle, Rachel works on setting goals. "When I first did my 'dream goal setting,' I was afraid to dream too far. But now that I've been involved with Circles this long—a year and a half—my dream goals have changed." Rachel feels very strongly about being involved in the Circles Campaign. "I want to be heavily involved in it in any way that I can by helping educate people to understand poverty and what it really is. My dream goal is really to work for Circles at some stage, whether it be on a national level or a local level." Rachel also wants to go back to college and to watch all of her children go as well. "I want to have them learn how to be successful. Maybe they won't have to go into poverty, but if they do, they will know how to get out."

A SENSE OF PURPOSE

After several years of being married to a man who was physically and mentally abusive, as well as addicted to drugs and alcohol, Eliza decided to make some changes. "I finally reached a point where I wanted to change my life and be the best mom for my two kids." Dealing with her own drug addiction, Eliza went through meetings, drug tests, and working with a caseworker to prove she was capable of being a good mother to her children. Her caseworker saw how much Eliza wanted to change and introduced her to a Circles Campaign.

When Eliza started attending Circles meetings, at first she went just to listen. "I was really nervous and didn't have much to say." It surprised her to be treated with respect. "What they gave me were choices. If I wanted to participate, I had a choice. If I wanted to say my name, it was my choice. If I wanted to tell my story, it was all a choice. It was really about building trust in a relationship." When people were nice to Eliza in the past, she always wondered what they wanted back from her. This experience opened her eyes to a new way of living. "I was able to see I had a lot in common with the people there, and I felt very safe."

Through people in the program, Eliza soon had two job opportunities. "It was amazing that I just met these people, and they automatically trusted me. They saw something in me that I didn't see, and I really needed that confidence." One big thing that changed in Eliza's life was her relationships with men. "For years I lost faith in men. I had so many bad experiences. My father was an alcoholic, and then my husband was abusive." Through the friendships with the men in her Circle, Eliza is now able to have trusting and open relationships with men. "This has helped me become a better person and a better mother to my son."

The men in Eliza's Circle wanted to help her with her children. One member is an advocate and a friend to her son. "My son needs a good positive role model in his life and needs attention." They also are spending time with her daughter to help her experience healthy relationships with men early in life. "This was a huge learning experience to have honest, caring men who will not let my family drop off the face of the earth. They want us to succeed, and they will help us."

After four years in her Circle while working the same job, Eliza's health deteriorated. "I had migraines, kidney stones, and infections. I didn't know why I got so sick all the time." She began to recognize that she couldn't do it all. "I started caring more about what was happening at my job than about my kids and myself. I became very chaotic, and I was blind to it." Her boss asked her to take a leave of absence due to health reasons with the assurance that, when she was ready to return, her job would be there for her.

"My Circle met with me and said I needed to get my priorities back together." Instead of telling her what to do, they asked what she needed. They gave her a choice, and because of this, she felt ready to make major changes. "I believe that we all were treading new ground, and we were all learning together. That was huge for me. I never felt like they were more powerful, but that we were on the same page doing things together."

Even though Eliza was involved in a Circle for more than four years, she had a hard time accepting help from other people. "I felt like I needed to fix everything myself. This was an idea that I held onto before I was in high school." She started to see the destruction this illusion of control was having on her life. "I was running my body to the ground. Because I was sick all the time, my children and my job didn't have me." Eliza now checks in daily with a Circle member to help her stay in touch with her priorities. "We have to make a plan. My depression really got hard when my health got worse and worse. It was debilitating. It could take me all day to convince myself I would be OK to pick my son up from school."

Eliza still has financial difficulties. "I'm broke, but my health is improving, so I can get ready to go back to work." She receives financial help when needed. "I have to ask and be in charge of my own finances. I am budgeting and it's working for me." She believes that Circles have helped with more than just getting her finances in order. "Poverty is very isolating. If I didn't have these relationships, I don't know where I would be." The relationships she developed enable her to live a full life. "My life before was based on a daily survival mode; I now have a sense of purpose."

DEVELOPING RELATIONSHIPS AND LEADERSHIP SKILLS

Rose is the mother of five children who has been part of a Circle for about two years. "I am one of those people with a very positive attitude with several goals, but I wasn't sure, with the things I needed to do, how to prioritize — how best to accomplish the goals." Rose has found that her Circle has helped her with the small and big things in her life. "When I first got my Circle, I was helping my mother with the end stages of her fight with ovarian cancer, and at the same time my husband had to leave and help with his father who had cancer." It was a very hard time in her life, so her Circle started helping by taking the kids to get haircuts for the funeral and other small things that were hard to do at the time.

"I'm the oldest of my siblings, so the responsibility of my mom's affairs landed on my shoulders, so [my Circle allies] were instrumental in counseling me in those things too." After her mother died, Rose found that she was the executor of her mother's estate, and she didn't have prior experience dealing with that amount of money. "I knew immediately that I could call my Circle and say what I thought needed to be done, and ask what they thought were appropriate steps to take."

Rose also has found that her Circle has helped how she sees herself. "It has helped me to go in different directions and to develop leadership skills." She has found that growth in the program is a progressive thing. "It's up to us to establish what our goals and needs are, and how much time we want to take, and how quickly we want to move." She has watched her leadership skills progress to the point that she now is a member of the board of directors for a community action organization. She would not have seen herself in this position before her involvement with Circles.

Some of the best things Rose gets out of being in a Circle are the relationships she has developed. "My community has grown, and other opportunities have opened up for me and my children that wouldn't have been present before." She found that she ended up building strong friendships with the people in her Circle. Rose's group has three allies; each one uses his or her own personal skills to help. "One person is really good with things in the community, and another is a more private person, so she likes to help me out with my finances." Her entire Circle gets together once a month, but Rose may meet with individuals if she needs help in other areas. "I have one gal in particular who is helping me with my résumé, and so we had a lunch meeting to look at that."

Rose has seen many changes in her life since being a Circle member. She has spent a lot of time on her finances. "We sat down with our Circle and did a cost comparison of daycare vs. me working full time." They looked at what benefits would be available from the state to help with daycare costs if she would have pursued working full time; she decided it would be a better option to stay at home. Things have been changing for her family. "My husband has moved up in pay, and now I'll have all of my five children in school full time." She looks forward to being able to return to the workforce.

Rose is very grateful to Circles and the community that she has formed. "I think it's an excellent program, and I'm very happy and pleased with how quickly and how much it has grown in our small community."

PART VI

Evaluate Options

In Story County, Iowa, and in many other areas of the United States, the vast majority of households do well financially. We have what we need, and can afford to spend our energy exercising our right to the pursuit of happiness. There is, of course, nothing wrong with the pursuit of happiness. But, to what extent can we close our eyes to the realities experienced by the many families—about 8,000 in Story County—who cannot afford the basic necessities of housing, transportation, food, heat, electricity, clothing, childcare, and medicine? How can we be fully happy while others are feeling marginalized, anxious, and financially desperate? Ultimately, how is it right that some of us can have everything we need and *most of what we want from the material world while others worry about evictions, utility shut-offs, and whether to pay for medicine or food?*

CHAPTER 13

Changing Our Choices Can Help End Poverty

We can tell ourselves that people must take responsibility to change their lives, get a job, and meet their basic needs. We can tell ourselves that people should not have children they can't afford, that they should keep their relationships going so they aren't trying to raise children alone, and that "deadbeat dads" should pay their child support. And we can tell ourselves that these problems are theirs and have nothing to do with us. Of course, we are right about all of this on some level. On another level, though, we all have some responsibility for ending persistent poverty. For many of us who are doing well, it's at least as much due to an accident of birth as to our own efforts.

There are both personal and institutional barriers that keep poverty in place for so many people. In Story County, about 8,000 families remain poor, and the children involved are growing up learning to have the same problems. We can tell ourselves that poverty has no effect on our pursuit of happiness, but we would be indulging in denial. All of us are affected by the poverty of others in some way, whether we realize it or not.

All children and teachers are affected when hungry or neglected children are unable to learn in our schools. Everyone is less safe in a community where some people don't have enough to meet their basic needs. When we reflect appropriately, we can be affected by feelings of guilt from enjoying what we do have while knowing that others can't afford decent meals.

The task of accomplishing change can feel entirely overwhelming! The good news is that there are many things each of us can do to contribute to ending poverty in our communities. Consider becoming a transformational leader to establish a Circles Campaign, thereby giving others living near you a chance to help one struggling family at a time. Then everyone can:

- By joining a Circle, be one of the "thousand points of light" that George H.W. Bush talked about during his presidency. Many in our society face mounting restrictions on access to limited assistance funding. These people need friendly contacts in the community as they find new ways to make ends meet.
- Donate a car. People need reliable transportation to get to school and work. In Story County, 160 cars were transferred over the course of a few years to families leaving welfare.
- Encourage those in your place of worship or civic organization to get involved to end poverty. Your local Circles Campaign can help you develop a simple and effective plan to engage your group in activities that will help reduce poverty in your community.
- Give generously to organizations that provide emergency cash assistance to families while promoting long-term self-sufficiency planning.
- Be alert to opportunities to help people around you out of isolation. People living in poverty often feel shame and so maintain distance from those having higher incomes. Invite people into your world. Bridge "the gap" to change your life and theirs for the better.

We must remind ourselves that no one needs to be left out in the cold and that everyone has a gift to give, although many may need to be asked to give it. Each of us can each add new meaning to our lives by finding a way to help someone so that he or she too can have enough to eat, be sheltered and clothed, and stop suffering in desperate financial circumstances.

Everyone in a community contributes in some way to the problem of poverty, and anyone can make a difference by committing to becoming part of the solution. Whether it be advocating for stricter laws to regulate payday lenders, increase affordable housing, and create more livable-wage jobs—or encouraging schools to transform so they can graduate more students each year—as an ally you can help to focus your community's attention on ending poverty.

Each of us can acknowledge a lack of money, meaning, or friendship in our own life, and then do something about it. We can choose to participate in community activities designed to strengthen everyone's foundation through mutual care and effort. Both decisions are important and necessary if we want to dismantle poverty.

We have identified many ways you can learn to become part of the eradication of poverty. You can help people get cars to go to work, to have enough nutritious food, to find affordable housing, to find affordable and safe childcare, or to find a livable-wage job with health benefits. You can become a friend who is there when needed. You can even give money to organizations that help when government programs can't.

Here are some suggestions about life habits and attitudes that may help as you begin to mobilize. Clearly this is a partial list that will not fit all people or all communities, but it can be used to stimulate further thought and discussion.

EXAMINE YOUR ATTITUDES CONCERNING SOCIAL PRIVILEGE

As is commonly done in most societies, we in the United States allocate power and privilege according to income level and competency. We align ourselves using assets and ability into a system we have usually referred to as a "class" system. In reality, of course, this system is simply a set of attitudes pertaining to levels of income and the amount of wealth controlled. To acknowledge these attitudes concerning society's "structure" is to take an important initial step toward ending poverty.

There are many ways we maintain the mental model that gives the most power and privilege to those with wealth. These few, whom we assign to the "upper middle class," seem to lack nothing. The "structure" proceeds from them in descending order: The labels we use are "middle class," "blue collar," "the poor." Far down on the privilege hierarchy are "the mentally ill" and "the poor who are mentally ill *and* homeless." Children rank just beneath the adults of each category.

We've constructed very detailed protocols for how much respect and privilege we give. The effects of these distinctions we make are very real for all of us—and can be especially devastating for individuals who have been convicted of felonies and those living with mental illnesses, learning disabilities, and physical challenges. The persistent effects of racism in our country have historically given a "white" more privilege than a "person of color." Similarly, we've given men more privilege than women, and middle-aged people more respect than either young or elderly people. Some of us even assign status to dogs and cats (with more than a few placing them well above certain categories of people), as well as to horses, rabbits, and other cute-looking animals. The ranking strategy proceeds downward toward those creatures perceived to be the very ugly and the very small.

As a "white" male from a middle-income family who did well in school and had his college expenses paid by others, I know about privilege. As someone whose early life experiences and choices led to a non-traditional career path, I also know what it is to feel marginalized by others—to feel as if you are less than others.

Although privilege feels better than being marginalized, these are two sides of the same coin: isolation on one side and a poverty of relationships on the other. To sustain a hierarchy of privilege requires perpetuation of the myth that some people should be included and other people should be left out of sharing in what is actually a finite reservoir of resources that should be available for the common good of everyone on Earth.

MANAGE MONEY WITH GREAT INTENTION

In most of the world, people are deprived of formal healthcare, adequate food, clean water, a safe home, and reliable transportation because they don't have enough money. People living in the United States earning incomes within the upper two-thirds range have far more than enough for what's needed to lead a healthy life. Spending money on things we don't need, or don't fully use, can feel bad for good reasons.

Making very conscious choices about spending money can reduce greatly the pressure of feeling a need to earn more and more. Our *unexamined mental models* compel us to buy more expensive homes, vehicles, vacations, clothes, and a seemingly endless list of other "stuff" to support lifestyle habits that require earning a high income, with all the attendant stress that can accompany doing so. Managing money with intention can free us from this spiraling trap.

To overspend, we have to tune out that part of our innermost selves that knows there are many in our immediate communities who don't have enough to meet even their most basic needs for survival. When we reflect on how that affects us all, we start making more conscious purchasing decisions, carefully assessing what we'll really gain from each new acquisition. We can consciously pause every day to remember that billions of people on Earth don't have enough money to meet their basic needs and that we are indeed privileged to have more than enough money for living our lives.

When we purchase an item that we don't appreciate and/or utilize to its fullest, we need to realize that we have just exchanged our *life energy* for something of no particular value. We earn money by using our most precious commodity—time. Managing money with great intention is an important way to honor our time in this world as the spiritual gift it is.

STAY AWARE OF WHAT TRULY SUSTAINS LIFE

Our lack of connection to the earth, coupled with our consumer might, is causing us to deplete our planet's finite resources. When we don't connect with nature on a regular basis, we can lose our sense of place. We can stop recognizing our utter dependence on Mother Earth for survival. This state of denial results in the kind of *poverty* stemming from both *a lack of spiritual nurture* (which derives from experiencing our natural world), as well as the *development of an increased reliance on material goods* for comfort.

RECOGNIZE YOUR PLACE IN THE CHAIN OF LIFE

To end poverty, individuals must begin to view all living things on Earth as important and worthy of respect. Decisions to change the environment, like building yet another mall or housing development, need to take into account any impact on the intricate system of life that must sustain us and our children's grandchildren. In the vast scheme of the universe, overindulgence on the part of a few at the expense of the many not only is immoral, it simply is not a road we can follow if our species is to survive.

CLAIM YOUR GIFTS AND DEVELOP A CIRCLE

Our world needs an antidote for the slow poison of isolation. To liberate ourselves from the uniform thinking that schools, media, fashion, and institutions of all kinds impose on us—to truly see our unique gifts and to figure out how to give them fully—we need a Circle of caring people to surround us with understanding, regular encouragement, and insight. By experiencing the power of a caring Circle of others, even the most challenged human being can find the inner strength and resources necessary to build a thriving life.

We can learn much by asking: What is the most meaningful contribution I can make to others and this world? What unique gifts do I have? These two fundamental questions can help guide us from childhood through our final days. By understanding and putting to use our unique individual gifts, which absolutely no one else can give, we participate in a mystery much bigger than ourselves—the "divinely chaotic" order of the universe.

APPRECIATE WHAT'S UNIQUE

Synthetic, processed uniformity sometimes seems to be taking over our nation. Millions of nearly identical homes are built and bought each year; the entryways to our towns are cluttered with aesthetically unappealing signs advertising the usual national and multinational corporate franchises; the quality of our media, and even our food, can assume a sameness that brings a certain numbness to our lives. By allowing such uniformity to dominate, we can sink into a *poverty of awareness,* blind to the inherently stunning beauty of our natural world and all of the unique people and creatures sharing time and space with us. It can feel hard to find this pristine perfection, lying as it so often does behind the onslaught of billboards, shrill radio talk shows, and concrete that we have allowed to so seriously infringe upon our forests and fields. Working to restore awareness restores the ability to let our natural gifts flow to help others.

HAVE FUN AS YOU EMBRACE LIFE IN ALL ITS WONDER

Being chronically deadly serious about society's great conundrums is antithetical to the life process. Each one of us is vastly interesting—as is a rainbow or even the tiny algae comprising "pond scum"! On some level, it is hilarious that what can bring fulfillment is right under our feet and only a touch away from the next human being, yet we can feel a need to travel to the moon and back looking for it. We need to savor our humanity *and* the earth while we go about saving it. The one who laughs *first* has more fun.

■ ■ ■

These ideas may inspire you . . . or not. They may cause a chain of events that move a mountain, or they may simply clarify disparate points of view. What is important is that I have honored the gift within me to write this chapter for you to read. It was the most meaningful act I could perform in this moment. Taking such action is transformational in and of itself. May we each do everything we can to establish a new mindset. It's up to each of us to take the time and invest the energy to tap our wells of personal skills and talents.

CHAPTER 14

Say Goodbye to Compromise

Poverty is perpetuated by compromises we make every day. Each community could find many opportunities to help alleviate poverty. For example, Iowa could invest more money to subsidize childcare programs. Ames has one of the least-affordable housing markets in the state. Iowa, one the biggest natural gardens on Earth, imports almost all of its food, and we pay the unnecessary freight costs. Thousands of families in our county have no health insurance: These breadwinners work full time, just as hard as those of us who have health insurance, but they can't see the doctor when the need arises.

Why aren't these problems fixed?

One of the main reasons we don't fix these problems is because so many of us are afraid to "rock the boat." People having middle-level incomes, who hold the majority of the total wealth of our economy, are mostly motivated by an emotional attachment to earning a certain amount of money: Indeed, for the most part, we aspire to become even wealthier. It seems that a common perception is that power is concentrated in the hands of individuals who have mega-resources. In fact, it is possible that Wall Street and politicians are more influenced by the large numbers of people in the middle than by the few with extreme wealth.

So we don't understand our true political power, either as individuals or as a group. Therefore, we compromise. We go along to get along.

Poverty exists when the majority, in the middle-income range, goes along with established company, industry, or political-party policies, even when these policies increase the cost of basic needs like housing, childcare, transportation, food, utilities, and healthcare.

I can think of two important examples of this in Iowa. We have allowed vast corporate agribusinesses to replace hundreds of smaller family farms. In addition, we have failed to keep suburban sprawl in check—a practice that often leaves an area resembling a donut, with most resources on the outside and poverty (in the original city or town) on the inside. All because of the money involved.

Those who understand what is happening too often don't speak up for fear of retribution from the companies they work for or from industry leaders. And so it goes, around our entire country and the world.

What if we became more rational in our thinking about money? We can all take steps to grow beyond the bad habit of compromising. Some of us can just give it up and see what happens—letting the cards fall where they fall. Lots of people survive on a lot less than most of us are used to having. Every day there are people who take the risk of experiencing temporary financial setbacks in return for gaining a deeper sense of integrity by telling the truth to expose what is hurting our communities.

Some of us can choose to pursue our own businesses and/or make a career change. Modern society is full of self-employment opportunities: Learning about these—and even carrying them out—is greatly facilitated by use of the Internet. Meeting with a career counselor may open doors for some. Exploring options can help us find new ways to tap our strengths to earn income. Even setting the stage to move on can sometimes make us feel bolder about speaking up for what we think is right.

We can pursue financial independence, which will eliminate our need to earn income. In other words, we can figure out how to retire early by changing the focus of our lives and our sources of income. In order to pursue more meaningful and fulfilling lives, thousands are choosing to live in a slower lane. By decreasing expenses and increasing savings, they are freeing themselves from having to earn money. As wise stewards of resources, they can turn more attention to being active community members. When earning enough interest income, one can choose to pursue any positive agenda, including doing more rewarding work and service in the community, without fearing the prospect of economic ruin. *Goodbye, compromise!*

Poverty won't end until enough of us in the middle take control of our spending, get out of debt, speak up about what we think is right, and stop compromising our values for the sake of potential income. Poverty is sustained in part by the high cost of basic needs. The cost of each of these needs can be reduced by the will of an informed and empowered community of caring people. We simply need to support each other to courageously do what is necessary to eliminate poverty so that every family has a realistic opportunity to thrive.

CHAPTER 15

Build True Financial Security to Be a Stronger Ally

To help others learn to become financially self-sufficient, first we need to develop the necessary skills ourselves. True financial security lies in acquiring a set of skills to manage money. In her book *You Don't Have to Be Rich*, Jeanne Chatzky cites research that revealed people are happier when they're firmly in control of their money, regardless of how much or how little they have. In other words, if you master skills for managing $20,000, you'll be happier than someone who earns $200,000 but doesn't have command of these financial skills.

There are five basic skills for handling money:

- Earning *enough* income
- Spending it wisely
- Saving
- Investing and trusting
- Giving money away and trusting life

EARN ENOUGH INCOME

Earning enough income requires determining how much money is enough to live on happily. Go to any library and look up books about personal finance. In any one of them you'll find a template for creating and recording a budget. Even with a guide, however, most people forget to write down *all* of their expenses. My wife and I found it helpful to commit to tracking expenses for 30 days. Then we compared what was actually spent to what I had thought we were going to spend. The former *was* higher than the latter. Knowing this difference helped us get our financial acts together.

Once you've determined a budget based on expense choices, you can set a goal for earning enough to support it. For example, if the amount you decide you need is $3,000/month, then your annual net-income need is $36,000. Add 30% more to pay taxes, bringing the total required to $46,800. Therefore, the annual income necessary to have enough money for $3,000/month in expenses might be $50,000, which leaves $3,200/year for savings.

This figure becomes a very important goal, because the brain goes to work once we give it an assignment. The mind is powerful and will help us achieve specific targets. If I know I need $50,000/year, then I will develop a $50,000 plan to earn it. If I think I need $30,000, then a $30,000 plan is set in motion. Of course, the goal also needs to feel feasible, so if I set the goal for $50,000 but sincerely believe that I cannot make that much money at this stage of life, then the mind will go with these stronger beliefs. Therefore, it's very important to set clear and *attainable* goals.

The process of setting and achieving a feasible income goal can be broken down even further. If I need $50,000 and currently earn $30,000, I need to increase my income by 66%. If, however, I'm earning $47,000, then I need to boost earnings by only 6.4%. These two scenarios involve forming completely different strategies. The first situation may require getting a new job, starting a business, going back to school, or perhaps taking on a second job. The second could be solved by getting a raise or a promotion—or picking up some nominal income on the side. If one has a clear and compelling vision of a goal, it *can* be accomplished. Most of us, needless to say, would need help to develop the "emotional muscles" necessary for believing that we deserve a 66% increase in income, no matter how much money that represents. Having support from others, especially those who already earn this much (or more), is essential for success.

Even though I've worked most of my life in nonprofit agencies, I have the strong conviction that I can and *should* make good money doing good things for my community and the world. I have never subscribed to the notion that people working in nonprofits should resign themselves to substandard pay. I've earned more income each year for the past 20 years, except the one year I relocated to Iowa to take a new job that had more long-term potential.

The following actions serve me well in achieving my goal to have enough money.

- Work out a specific target number for income
- Research the market price of my work
- Ask for what I want
- Partner with people who will support my financial goals
- Take appropriate development steps
- Do not push the process faster than it can happen

It has helped to stay on the same career path for 25 years. This decision has brought a deeper knowledge of my field, a wider circle of contacts, and a set of skills vital to securing contracts and grant awards when opportunities present themselves.

SPEND WISELY

There truly can be great joy in frugality. Spending consciously means considering the real importance of each purchase before buying. Anytime we can eliminate a line item from our budget—or decrease its amount on a permanent basis—we are, in effect, giving ourselves a lifelong raise in pay. (For example, people who successfully quit smoking suddenly have a significant amount of disposable income they didn't have before.) The less we need to spend to be happy, the smaller will be the "nest egg" required for financial independence and freedom from the necessity to work only for pay.

In the book *Your Money or Your Life*, Joe Dominguez and Vicki Robin advocate evaluating your spending at the end of each month in terms of whether or not it was in alignment with your values. Then they recommend using the same process to determine whether the amount spent on various items during the following month should be more, less, or stay the same.

My wife and I have been tracking expenses for several years. We have a very simple budget. Every month we have a "business meeting" to decide how much money to include for each line item. We try to get as close to our target as we can—or, better, come in even lower than we originally thought we could. By now, we've become quite good at estimating each line item and meeting our goals. To have control over spending helps reduce stress. It means that no matter how much money we have coming in, we know how to control spending in order to live within our means. Spending wisely is just as important as earning enough.

My wife and I have developed a much stronger commitment to this process over time. At first I was much more interested in tracking and reviewing expenses than she was. But now that she no longer *needs* to work and can see how much I want financial independence, her enthusiasm for, and abilities with, the process have increased steadily. She is now very skilled at keeping us both on track with our intentions.

I developed a spreadsheet that lists each line item and projects an amount for every month of the year. At the end of each month, I replace the projections with actual amounts and note the differences. I also calculate how much money I can put into savings when spending goes up or down each month. Any change in this amount provides instant feedback on how long it will take to become financially independent. I also can experiment by adjusting annual spending and saving rates. Usually I make the assumption that both the current and future rate of return on savings will be a minimum of 5%. While future interest-income figures are projections, our current spending rate and "nest egg" size are real figures. They provide us with sufficient motivation to reach our goals.

The primary questions to ask about spending are:

- Do we really need it to be happy?
- Can we do it ourselves?
- Have we worn out what we already have?
- Can we do without it for 30 days and then see if we still really want it?

Often our impulses to buy more "stuff" go away with time. Most of the time it actually makes us happier to watch our savings grow and our monthly spending shrink.

The big-ticket items—cars, homes, and education—are the most important budget decisions to scrutinize. Saving big money on these big expenses will greatly facilitate the realization of financial goals.

Sometimes what initially looks like more can turn out to be less. When we first moved to Ames in 1998, we bought a starter home near the university campus. It was the most affordable home we could find that was also charming and livable. However, we underestimated the impact of problems arising from living in close proximity to 25,000 students and so decided to sell 13 months later. We moved downtown into a home that cost 50% more than the first one; but within a year of being downtown, we realized we could let go of one of the cars, thereby saving $5,000/year in auto expenses. This fact alone would pay for the difference in the prices of the two homes over a 10-year period.

Spending wisely also means paying off debts as soon as possible. Credit card balances usually carry higher interest rates than other debts—often much higher. These were the first on our list of loans to eliminate. We haven't paid interest on a credit card for more than 10 years because we make it a priority to pay off the balance each month. In fact, we learned to prioritize debt elimination according to interest rate. Our goal was to pay off our debts by proceeding from the ones with highest to the ones with lowest rates. When we first moved to Iowa, we had student loans, two car loans, a loan on a ring I bought my wife, and some credit card debt. Eight years later we had finally eliminated all these debts and now carry only our mortgage.

We also discovered that spending consciously is more important than the specific benchmarks we reach. True financial security comes from knowing how to *be in charge* of how much we spend, as well as from buying only what we really want or need.

SAVINGS

It seems to me there are three reasons to save money:

- To have an emergency reserve
- To be able to pay for large purchases, like a car, with cash
- To build a "nest egg" that eventually generates enough interest income to live on

It took us awhile to understand how important it is to have money automatically taken from my paycheck each month for deposit into my savings account, as promoted by David Bach in his book *The Automatic Millionaire.* For us, this has proved to be an exceptionally valuable tool.

In addition, we automatically deposit the maximum allowed amount into Roth IRAs from my paycheck each month. We have the maximum amount allowed for tax-deferred savings automatically deposited into a 401(k). At the end of each month, any excess funds are placed into yet another savings account, then used to invest regularly. We have a money-market fund for cash we might need quickly, certificates of deposit (CDs) for money we might want in the short run, annuities for safe long-term investments, and mutual funds that range from high to low risk.

No matter what our income has been, we have learned that we can probably find a way to save money. Having clear goals is the key. After eliminating all of our debts except the mortgage, we saved the equivalent of three months of income as a cash reserve. We received several thousand dollars from the sale of our home before moving to Ames, which provided a start for this reserve. After one of our cars was involved in an accident, we decided to replace it with a much less expensive used car, freeing up another large amount of money. As a result, we currently carry a cash-reserve fund that can cover six months of living expenses.

INVEST WISELY AND TRUST ADVICE

Since I am not a financial planner, I'm not qualified to offer specific tips on investing. I have learned, to my regret, that financial planners vary widely in their knowledge, wisdom, and accessibility. Investing requires a commitment from us to earn more than we spend. It also requires obtaining an education regarding investment risks and rewards—and to find an advisor who is trustworthy. My wife and I are currently working with a group that specializes in socially responsible alternative investments.

The more precisely I can identify what risks I can tolerate, which ones I can't tolerate, and my goals and expectations, the better job I'll do as a partner with my financial planner. We can feel more positive about life when our values are in alignment with those of the companies in which we invest our financial resources. We hope to see our investments grow by an average of 6–8% per year during the next eight years. To do that we'll make regular savings deposits and rely on someone we can trust to guide our investment choices, so we can ultimately reach our larger goal of becoming financially independent.

WORK TOWARD FINANCIAL INDEPENDENCE

Save $500,000, invest it for a return of 5%, and $2,000 will show up in your bank account each month. Learn how to be happy living on $2,000/month, and you now are free from the necessity of working for pay. Too hard to save $500,000? Find some career counseling to learn how you can earn more money per hour. Still seems too hard? Learn how to live on $1,500/month and decrease your saving target.

Building a "nest egg" is all about self-esteem, supportive relationships, and, as mentioned earlier, making automatic deposits each month. The key is to fix your mind on the goal of financial independence. When we can see ourselves in the best light, have ample support for taking a new step, and learn from relationships with people who earn more money, our lives can change for the better.

GIVE AWAY MONEY AND TRUST LIFE

There is something almost magical that happens to me when I give money away. It seems to me that giving money away keeps it in its proper perspective. Giving away money affirms my knowledge that there is more where that came from and my faith that I will receive more in the future. Giving away money increases my sense of self-meaning. It is a paradox: The more I give, the more I receive.

Giving away money means that I trust the life process. It is in my nature to give; I believe this is true for each of us. The reason that the saying "It is better to give than to receive" is true is because *in the act of giving I let go of fear.* I have to let go of money and trust that life will provide a return on that investment. I can gain just as much satisfaction from this as I can from examining the growing balance on a mutual-fund statement.

To put one's trust in money saved is ultimately unsound. True financial security and stability are gained from understanding the principles discussed above, which are summarized here:

- We each deserve to earn enough money to thrive—and a bit more than that to save.
- We can spend money consciously on only those things and activities that nurture us according to our values, in ways that don't create the unnecessary stress of living beyond our means.
- Saving money creates a strong base of energy that we can draw on to pursue the life of our dreams.
- Wise investment of our money can eventually create an adequate reserve that generates a "living wage" interest income.
- By being generous we show others we know that all is well—and that all *will be* well.

Applying these money skills will build financial security. We can begin at any time in life, with whatever money we have.

PART VII

Become the Change You Want to See

Many of us feel destined to help usher in a new era in which each individual is as important as every other individual and is treated accordingly; we each form a more intimate relationship with Earth, our home from which we cannot escape; and we understand that we must treat the earth as a sacred entity that is worthy of tireless care.

While many of us think we should *work to accomplish these changes, very few actually know* how *to do this. That is why we must join together to learn from the* transformational leaders *among us. We then need to become intentional about teaching their successful strategies to those who develop a passion for working toward establishing healthier belief systems and more sustainable lifestyles.*

CHAPTER 16

Accept a New Direction

The elimination of poverty will require most of us to make some radical shifts in our fundamental understandings of reality and our accepted systems of belief. For some, the most basic changes will involve the way in which we view our relationship to other people and to the planet that is our collective home. We need to recognize that we are in constant and obligatory interrelationship with every other human being, with Earth, and with everything in the universe. In this framework of understanding, assaults on our environment will be seen as actual assaults on our individual selves. Whatever we are doing now is of the utmost importance to our collective future. Good ends *never* justify bad means. We will always reap what we sow.

It is unconscionable to abuse the earth. It is unconscionable to tolerate poverty. Imagine the possibilities if we all worked to achieve the concept of Heaven on Earth—right here, right now.

We have *unlimited* talents to use to transform our individual lives, our communities, and our societies. All human beings are just as important as all other human beings. All manifestations of nature are worthy of our respect and attention. Seeing reality in this way will give us the power to end poverty and at the same time bring about a sustainable relationship with our environment. Our deepest passions for Heaven can be fully realized in our lives here on Earth. We can learn how to enable people who live in poverty to contribute their unique gifts to the world. Respect for the environment will provide new ideas so we can halt our abuses, allowing the earth to heal. We can banish poverty from our own country, then together turn our attention to helping the poorest nations in the world build strong, self-sustaining economies.

Humanity is poised to undergo transformational changes that will lead toward a deep compassion for our environment and profound, respectful relationships among all the world's people. Move the Mountain Leadership Center is inspiring and equipping organizational leaders to help usher in the transformations that seem imminent in this country. Using a deliberate, loving, and determined process to identify, prepare, and support our transformational leaders, we can develop society's capacity to embrace the gifts of all, empower the marginalized to engage fully in societal life, and build a sustainable relationship with our Earth.

CHAPTER 17

Work for Societal Changes to End Poverty

Once enough of us consciously shift our priorities, it will be possible to pursue many more solutions to alleviate poverty. In this section I will briefly outline a few common-sense approaches.

- **Encourage educators to teach children financial literacy in our schools.** There are two languages that everyone needs to be at least familiar with in order to succeed in this country: English and Money. Since we live in a capitalistic economic system, let's teach everyone how it works. Let's teach everyone how to make and manage money. If you don't know the difference between an asset and a liability, you'll buy liabilities and have no assets to show for your hard work. We need to learn how to enjoy what we have—and to want mostly what we need—to avoid exceeding the emotional and physical limits of our ability to pay for goods and services. *There is no need to consume ourselves to death.*

- **Go out of your way to build new relationships in the Circles Campaign.** You can encourage everyone to do whatever it takes to help others earn more income, so that everyone can afford to pay his or her own expenses. A good way for many people to do this is to join a Circles Campaign. Corporate gifts, donations, membership fees, and innovative government programs will provide funds to finance these initiatives. Once established, each Circles Campaign convenes a monthly Big View meeting so that transformational leaders in business, government, human services, and faith organizations can gather for discussions to ascertain what it would take for families in their local community to leave poverty behind. Once committed, community leaders can work to create:

- Affordable housing, transportation, childcare, and healthcare
- Livable-wage jobs
- Equitable tax codes
- The revitalization of neighborhood life

Ending poverty means:

- Helping individuals change
- Changing how we provide services
- Eliminating policy disincentives
- Generating more economic opportunity
- Doing away with victimizing practices, such as predator lending

Remember, major transformations are needed—not mild fixes. It's good to plan for long-term efforts (on the order of 20 years) to make these necessary changes.

- **We can all work to help create a universal health insurance system** that promotes individual responsibility. We need to pay more attention to eating better, exercising, and getting regular check-ups. We need to consider the possibility of allowing natural death with dignity to occur, instead of feeling compelled to lose a lifetime's savings in order to eke out a few more days or weeks spent in illness. Half of all bankruptcies are caused by medical costs, and most of these are incurred during the final days and weeks of life. *We need to invest in prevention rather than paying so heavily after health deteriorates irreversibly.* We need to vigorously question our healthcare industry, in which a very few people make a great deal of money.

- **We can work to blend existing welfare assistance with individualized plans** that may, in many cases, make better sense. Cutting off childcare and health insurance subsidies before an individual can replace this support through an employer's health insurance program is putting the cart before the horse. This can't help anyone become self-sufficient and, in the end, actually *is more costly,* since now more tax dollars are required to maintain subsidies longer than would have been necessary otherwise.

■ **We need to work toward the goals of increasing high school graduation rates and making college affordable for everyone.** According to recent U.S. Census Bureau data, the average annual income for those who did not graduate from high school is $22,969; for those with a high school diploma, $28,816; and for those having a bachelor's degree, $52,462. It's difficult to imagine how, five years from now, young adults will be able to make their way into livable-wage jobs without a *college* degree. How will *anyone* escape poverty five years from now without a high school diploma? *We need to support secondary-school systems toward the goal of having 100% high school graduation rates—and do what it takes to retool the education culture so that all students are truly prepared for success in the world.*

■ **We need to start building affordable housing again.** These days we're building homes larger than 2,000 square feet. People in the bottom half of our economy simply can't afford them. In the recent past we lived comfortably in 1,200-square-foot homes. We need to encourage a trend for the future toward smaller communities of energy-efficient, mixed-priced, and mixed-density housing developments, which will have the added benefit of providing opportunities to get to know one's neighbors through the use of sidewalks, porches, and alleys. We can resist the current trend of living in isolated, gated enclaves comprising massive houses distant from shops. These tend to lessen a sense of community (even within the enclosure) and often require residents to drive greater distances—to the detriment of the environment. *We need to work toward creating housing communities in this country that are energy-efficient and affordable.*

■ **We need to increase wages** so people don't have to work two full-time jobs to make ends meet. The trend toward globalization and the growing income gap between the wealthy and everyone else have presented numerous challenges in this regard, but our nation is capable of buffering these changes. *Anyone working full time should easily be able to afford the basic necessities of life.*

■ **Local economic impact studies** need to be conducted and utilized for all new business development, in order to ensure that our communities do not end up subsidizing profitable but low-paying employers, who can ultimately require actual additions to the publicly-paid social service infrastructure to support their employees. We need to avoid creating situations in which *more* tax revenue is needed to support *new poverty* generated by the introduction of low-wage jobs into the community!

■ **We all need to do whatever is necessary to help families stay together.** A single parent earning today's minimum wage *cannot*, without assistance, provide adequately for a child. If the current 50% divorce rate continues as the norm, we're likely to continue to see a rising poverty rate. People learn most of what they know about partnering and parenting at home. For the most part, these basic skills are passed from generation to generation. Unfortunately, what is actually being passed down by 50% of today's families is a legacy of separation and increasing poverty. Children, youth, and adults need much more *formal education* about how to create and sustain healthy family relationships.

■ **We need to devise federal taxation policies that are just and pragmatic.** Too often extreme wealth is undertaxed—or even *un*taxed—while those earning middle and lower incomes support the bulk of our social infrastructure. This is both unfair and impractical. *A strong democratic society depends on the presence of a large group of people earning middle-level incomes.*

■ **Communities, states, and federal agencies need to seek leadership development** in order to move from the "grants management" business model into a "community building" model. Anti-poverty organizations will be most effective when they engage the community in strategies that help individual families out of poverty. It is an all-too-common mistake to assume that "the poor" are being taken care of by "the system." Each of us needs to strive to *become part of* a transformed and more effective society, however we can.

■ ■ ■

Poverty will end when enough of us realize that we can and should end it. The most important thing each of us can do is to examine our own assumptions, along with the choices we make, to see how we currently influence the status quo (for better or for worse). Promoting and working toward any of the goals presented above will help. If we are committed, if we have regular discussions about how to proceed, and if we follow through by acting on good ideas, we *can* eventually end poverty.

CHAPTER 18

Organizational Leadership Training for an Emerging New Mindset

Birthing a new societal belief system is a profound and difficult challenge. *Transformational leaders* play a key role in changing belief systems. Many organizational leaders become less effective at achieving true transformation because after a while the job can seem impossible. Many assume that they can't bring about dramatic new results, so they resign themselves to management activities rather than using vital leadership skills that are required to align others with a powerful vision.

Move the Mountain Leadership Center, with sponsorship from the Annie E. Casey Foundation, interviewed the directors of community leadership programs in Chicago, Cleveland, Los Angeles, Phoenix, and San Diego. These conversations revealed that current community leadership training programs tend to provide elemental components but don't provide what's needed to inspire organizational leaders to commit to the long and significant change processes that transform society—to become transformational leaders.

Move the Mountain Leadership Center's training experience with organizations also has shown that as leaders:

- We're too isolated. We lack sufficient training and don't have adequate ongoing coaching that can result in major change.
- We often can't say exactly where we're taking people. Plans are imprecise and often not ambitious enough.
- We don't communicate urgency. The problems we confront are enormous, but we demonstrate too much complacency to generate necessary solutions.

- We manage more than we lead. We don't know how to delegate the business of management in order to turn enough of our attention to accomplishing change.
- We don't have a clear roadmap to help understand the process of change. Therefore, we declare victory before change is embedded, or we abandon the process when self-doubts become too difficult to manage.

Everywhere one looks there is evidence of institutionalized ennui caused by inadequate organizational leadership. The results of this void are all around us:

- Global warming
- Chronic poverty
- Random acts of violence in our schools
- Escalating crises in major national systems like healthcare, transportation, housing, energy, and education.

When we do find high-functioning organizations that are growing and developing over time, we find strong leaders who *understand the process* of leading transformational change.

Move the Mountain Leadership Center has developed a training and consulting program to help individuals step into the role of transformational leader. Past participants report that the efforts they've put into this training process have paid off for years afterward. Our course is described in more detail on pages 126 through 131.

PART VIII

Step Onto a Spiritual Path

W*hy* are *we here anyway? Are we spiritual beings having an earthly experience, or are we earthly beings seeking a spiritual promise? It is clear to me that we are something more than our thoughts, our homes, our possessions, our friends, and our work. If we can pursue a higher purpose—a path other than one simply leading to the accumulation of more wealth—we will develop qualities that will bring more joy and meaning to our lives.*

CHAPTER 19

Take the Larger View

In this section I will try to summarize and tie together some of the broad ideas presented earlier in the book, with the hope that having such a list may help guide planning or stimulate further reading and discussion.

- **Make good friends.** Everyone needs at least a few really good friends. Build close connections with several people who can be counted on to help with an unexpected crisis at 3 o'clock in the morning. *Be sure to call* if the crisis can't wait until daybreak. Reaching out for help when you need it can build a bridge that will remain in place for your friend's time of need.

- **Nurture your friendships.** People in our country look very lonely to those living in cultures that value community more than individual wealth. To decrease loneliness and isolation, live in a neighborhood with sidewalks and front porches rather than a gated community with a 2-acre zoning code. Or . . . stay behind the gate, but break the mold and build significant relationships with your neighbors. Friends need to know they *are* our friends. An invitation to a simple meal, to watch a movie together, or to play tennis helps let someone know you value their part in your life, no matter what their income may be relative to your own. When invited to share some time with a friend, make the time to do so. This lets a person know that you can be depended upon—that you won't disappear when the going gets tough.

- **Safeguard your health.** Many health problems can be alleviated or even avoided by taking charge of a few simple things. Exercising regularly, eating right, getting enough rest, drinking plenty of water, and getting regular physicals will help keep our health optimal. Illness can be complicated, expensive, uncomfortable, time-consuming, and more. Can't get motivated to live a healthier lifestyle? Hire a personal trainer, join an exercise class, or team up with an experienced friend. Find that partnership, and hurry out the door!

- **Heal family wounds.** Carry the best of your family's strengths forward into the future. Think hard about whether staying upset or angry with your parents, siblings, children, or other relatives is worth the effort involved and the effect on your life. No matter what the perceived offense, work toward a resolution within yourself. After all, your family is yours for life. If you find no enjoyment in the relationship whatsoever, do what you have to do to avoid being manipulated and move on with your life, carrying the lessons learned with you.

- **Find a hobby.** Everyone is talented in more than one way. Find an affordable hobby, then enjoy it as often as possible. If it's an activity you can share with others, it will increase happiness and reduce isolation.

- **Be generous as you work to achieve financial independence.** Save for the future, and remember to build generosity toward others into your financial plan. See what a difference you can make by sharing some of your discretionary income directly with someone in need. Again, I've found that the more I give, the more I receive.

- **Remove clutter from your life!** Having more than we can use is oppressive. Unnecessary possessions weigh on the mind and soul—and can decrease happiness.

- **Share the load.** All of us have been affected by growing up in a culture with plenty of distress patterns. We all have daily opportunities to feel bad about ourselves. As needed, get regular counseling from someone who knows what they're doing. We all can take advantage of professional expertise to help work through times when we get stuck. And find friends you trust to listen to you and your concerns. Listen as well to theirs, or "pay it forward" by listening to someone else who needs a compassionate ear.

■ **Play more than you think you should play.** Have more fun. Make a list of things you love to do, then do them regularly. If you allow yourself the freedom to play, you'll discover that you're more efficient and effective. You'll return to your work with more enthusiasm—and may even find that your mind was productive as you played. Solutions to problems sometimes occur to us when we focus for a while on something unrelated. Playing more can help give you a sense of having more control over your own life.

■ **Enjoy nature.** If you don't already have a relationship with the great outdoors, create one. *We are connected to the earth!* To pretend otherwise is hard on the soul. So . . . take a walk in the woods, look at the stars, grow something, plant a tree, pick some flowers, and appreciate how amazing it all is.

■ **Have regular "business" meetings with your significant other.** It isn't too much to ask for weekly breakfast meetings (maybe at the local café?) about the big issues that come up in every intimate relationship—money, family, sex, and health, to name a few. What do you want? What does your partner want? What can be done to make both of you happy?

■ **Make a list of the feelings that are most important to you,** then organize your activities and relationships to encourage those feelings. Harmony? Freedom? Adventure? Financial peace of mind? Mastery? A sense of belonging? Keep this list nearby in a notebook as a regular reminder of what's really important in life. Organize and meet once a month with a "goals support group." Structure and accountability go a long way toward accomplishing almost anything.

■ **Save the earth.** If you can, have only one vehicle. Cars are expensive and a major source of air pollution. Take the bus, carpool, walk, bike, or work out of your home. If you need two cars, make sure they get good mileage and use them wisely.

Give careful thought to how your activities affect the environment. According to the Ecological Footprint Network, it now takes more than one year and two months for our planet to regenerate what we take from it during a single year. As detailed in the Report on Global Warming released in February 2007, scientists from all nations have reached consensus about the fact that our consumption patterns pose a very serious threat to the biological systems required to sustain human life on Earth.

The good news is that individuals can take important steps to change this situation. It isn't necessary to overconsume. Many organizations provide useful suggestions for bringing lifestyles into better balance with the environment. We can each help preserve our intricate ecosystems to ensure that *our* grandchildren will be able to know and love *theirs.* There may be other places somewhere in space that could sustain life, but solving the problems we have on *this* planet seems to be a more prudent course of action than expecting to relocate outside our solar system.

- **Provide the leadership to end poverty.** In this country those earning in the bottom third of our economy support and provide services for those earning in the top two-thirds. For me, it is simply unconscionable that the folks in this third of our population are unable to fully support families as they work to take care of hotel rooms, serve coffee, checkout groceries, and clean up lawns and buildings. Working together, we can end poverty in networks of communities focused on accomplishing this within the next two generations.

■ ■ ■

If you work to be happier, make friends, end poverty in your community, and save our environment, you will automatically be perceived as a leader—an example of what is possible. Life can be very hard. But it doesn't have to be miserable and small. Let your life inspire and equip others to become happier.

MORE THAN JUST DAY-TO-DAY LIVING

One of the hardest things for Andrea about living in poverty was how it affected her children. "We would get the school supplies that they needed, but new clothes and shoes were very limited." One day her 7-year-old came home from school and told her that another child was making fun of him. He said, "This kid keeps telling me that my momma gets my clothes out of the garbage can." Andrea told her son to either ignore the boy or tell him that it wasn't true. Her son replied, "I know Mom, but it hurts. The other kids laugh at me." This was hard for Andrea because she couldn't fix that hurt for her son. "I felt angry and sad that I couldn't get my family out of the situation we were in."

Andrea, her husband, and their four children worked very hard at making ends meet before they found Circles. "We lived in public housing in a part of town that we called 'the projects.' " Andrea was working in a local convenience store for $5.15/hour. "We were living paycheck to paycheck." The first thing in the morning Andrea would think about was how they were going to deal with what the day would give them. "With the children it isn't just about getting food on the table: I also have to worry about their health. We don't have any benefits working minimum wage, so if your child gets sick it means that I miss a day of work." That day of work for Andrea made a huge difference in her paycheck and would really affect the quality of her family's life for the month.

Despite their very low income, they learned how to find help for their children. "We were on food stamps and Medicaid and lived in public housing where our rent was based on our income." Even with this help, there were many financial burdens on the family of six. "We had to pay the electricity and gas bill. We didn't have a car, so we walked everywhere we had to go." Andrea's family spent a lot of time together. "My kids had the roof over their heads and food in their bellies, but we didn't do activities out in the community; our time was at home. We didn't watch much TV because we only had one channel, and my husband and I made a lot of time for the kids." At the end of the day Andrea would feel tired, run down—hopeless. "We just lived day to day without any big goals for our lives."

Andrea met people through her children's programs who changed her life. "We had two very inspiring people from Head Start that kept saying I should go back to school and really believed in me." Andrea didn't think going back to school would be possible because of her four children, but after a lot of persuasion, she decided it would be best for her family. "It was very hard and interesting to work all of this out."

For her program, she was required to spend 40 hours doing a practicum with a community program. She found a position with the director of community development in her county. Through this job, she learned about Circles.

"My boss asked me if I would be the first Circle member in our county. I said yes, not even knowing what it was about." When Andrea brought this idea home to her husband, he didn't think it would be a good idea. "My husband thought that if you tell people in the community that we're struggling to take care of our four children, they would take the kids away. He didn't think it would be smart to tell people our problems."

Through Andrea's job, she started working to get Circles going in their county. She helped to send out letters and worked on planning the kick-off. "It was a big task. I felt like it was awesome that I got to be involved in all of it." In each county that Andrea and the Circles organizers visited, Andrea spoke about her life. "The mayor patted me on the back and told me he was proud of the way I was changing." Her husband also decided to join Circles because he noticed that Andrea was changing from her old way of living. "He saw me working hard, and I wasn't stressing about the bills. My attitude had changed."

One of the first things Andrea and her husband did as leaders of a Circle was to look at the financial decisions they were making. "Tax time came up, and we shared what we normally do with our financial ally." Usually they would go to an accountant and pay $200 extra to get the return back on the same day. "We asked him if it was OK, and he told us that paying money for a rapid refund was throwing it away." Their ally also led them to resources for filing their own taxes. "He gave us a disk that he can download onto your computer and will print the papers, and you're done; and all you have to pay for is a stamp." This was important financial information that they didn't have in the past.

Andrea's life has changed drastically. "During this time I've managed to graduate from college, maintain a car, and move from public housing to a six-bedroom, two-bath house." They're in the process of finishing a homebuyers' class to learn all the steps of buying the house they now live in. "Hopefully by the end of the year the house will be ours." They're also more involved with their children's school. "We're not ashamed to go to the school functions. Before, I was ashamed to—you know, the way my kids were dressed. I couldn't give my kids the fancy clothes."

Being in a Circle also has changed Andrea's children. "Their attitude is so much better, and they're not ashamed of themselves." She sees now that they're more in touch with their emotions. "They show their feelings, and they're more involved in school." The children love Circles so much that they beg to go. "We have foster grandparents that come in and sit in the child room, so they call them 'Grandma.' "

Andrea has been especially happy about her life changes because this is the first year as a parent that she has actually given her kids a good Christmas. "My children got a lot of gifts and also learned to give back." They adopted a family, and the kids helped pick out gifts for them. "They loved it. They took them shopping, and it seemed like they were more excited buying the other kids gifts than getting their own."

Even though she didn't think it would have been possible, Andrea is working toward an administrative position in her job. "I have goals, and I've been shown that I can do anything I want to do. Anything." Andrea now describes her life as amazing. She says that being in a Circle has made her family more aware of things to the point where they feel they can pass what's been learned on to other people. "[Our allies] have given us the meaning of life, friendship, community, family. They've taught us a lot." Financially, Andrea and her husband are now above the poverty level, but emotionally and physically she doesn't feel as if they're completely out yet. "We're not quite ready to be allies. But I perceive that by the end of the year we'll be ready to move on."

PART IX

For Our Children's Grandchildren

Join me for a moment on a journey through time to my vision for the future.

CHAPTER 20

Ending Poverty by 2050

When I woke up on January 1, 2050, I joined my large circle of friends to celebrate formally the elimination of poverty from Story County, Iowa. Let me tell you how this happened. It's an amazing story that few believed possible 40 years ago.

In 2050 a lot of money from our cities, the county, places of worship, and individuals has been used to solve the underlying problems of poverty.

Once we accomplished taking care of our children, then, and only then, did we turn our attention to personal issues of convenience and preference. Schools no longer charge fees for extracurricular activities. All children now have access to computers in the home so that the playing field is level from the beginning.

We helped children decide to postpone having children. Adults made the conscious decision to slow down and to take the time to really notice the extraordinary individuality of each child in our community. We decided to invest more of our time and energy in raising our children than in the pursuit of wealth. We got so interested in children that we were right there for them, in appropriately sensitive ways, on the very days when they had questions about sexuality, feelings of loss, and anxieties about being loved. We got more sophisticated about what children need from adults and made it our priority to give it to them. We watched while teen births gradually decreased, then became a thing of the past. During 2049 in Story County no child was born to teenaged parents.

Adult parents in Story County learned how to value maintaining a committed relationship above all else—and how to simplify life by reducing unnecessary consumption, freeing up time and energy for building and strengthening their commitment. We realized that the benefits of having a successful lifelong partnership far outweigh the difficulties we all experience sustaining one. People stopped tolerating emotional and physical abuse—indeed, the community developed strong, assertive plans to interrupt patterns of abuse in families. Men and women realized the necessity of establishing good friendships in order to stay close to their partners. People got better about asking friends for help with negotiating the challenges of staying together and raising a family. Children observed these changes, and so learned how to choose compatible mates and how to communicate effectively to maintain a good intimate relationship. The rate of family break-ups fell from 50% to 6%.

Employers in Story County saw the wisdom of turning away from short-term earnings, investing more time and money into building teams of steady, reliable, well-paid workers able to fully utilize their talents to provide meaningful services to the community. During the past 40 years there has been a decisive shift away from generating products and services of questionable value for people and the environment toward a deep commitment to enrich lives while conserving and renewing natural resources for future generations.

Health insurance was recognized as a basic human right and became universally accessible, benefiting thousands of vulnerable families in Story County. Many of the county's older residents still remember the years of preferential medical care; younger people hear those stories with disbelief.

Transportation changed as radically here as in the rest of the nation. Electric vehicles replaced the fleet of polluting cars we once had. These are recharged by plugging into household outlets connected to the power "grid" that is now generated nationwide by regional hydroelectricity projects, wind turbine "farms," and the widespread use of solar panels. Supplementation of our clean energy supply by natural gas-burning facilities is necessary less than 5% of the time. Electric bus service now extends to all area businesses and communities. The use of bicycles increased dramatically as it became safer and easier to pedal around the county on hundreds of miles of newly constructed bike paths. As generosity and making new friends became a normal way of life, carpooling became easy. People with lower incomes now don't have to worry about maintaining a car. There are plenty of ways to get where one needs to go. Those who absolutely need a car but can't afford the price can obtain a vehicle that has been donated.

The cost of housing decreased dramatically during the last 40 years. No one now has to spend more than 30% of take-home pay for rent. The city of Ames and Story County, through a number of bold public initiatives, paved a clear and reasonable path for anyone to obtain, then move from, affordable, subsidized rental situations to home ownership.

Since adults were more focused on children, there was much enthusiasm for creating the best childcare support we could. Iowa has joined the rest of the states in providing excellent and affordable childcare for all. Adults became more thoughtful about when to have children—and how many to have—vastly reducing the sense of desperation felt by many parents in the past over lack of childcare availability. Most people had more time to spend with their own children because of their commitments to staying together as families and, as life became more affordable and manageable, not feeling compelled to work ever-longer hours.

Story County developed such a powerful social safety network that it became virtually impossible for anyone to suffer poverty in isolation. These emergency financial support services have become just as important to us as our emergency fire and police services. People in our communities now know when families are in financial trouble and so are able to reach out quickly and effectively before evictions, job losses, family break-ups, and a host of other destructive outcomes occur. Every community has ample emergency funding, plenty of skilled volunteers and professionals who know how to intervene, and Circles to ensure that people don't fall back into poverty. A family's financial crisis is treated as an opportunity for community members to reach out in service to a neighbor—to support a family out of isolation. We have realized that every member of the community has gifts to share, and we've stopped wasting human potential by marginalizing individuals and families living in poverty.

When I woke up on January 1, 2050, I realized that at some point during the past 40 years a critical mass of people had figured out how to have enough money, enough friendship, and enough meaning in their lives to be truly happy. This core group became the catalyst necessary for making it an eventual reality for everyone. Story County had been transformed.

BACK TO THE PRESENT

My vision may or may not become a reality. It's really up to us. I am committed to reaching the goals presented in this book, and so are many others. *You* can make a big difference in someone's life. It *is* possible to eliminate poverty.

■ ■ ■

May peace be with you: May your children inherit a thriving Earth, may your neighbor rise safely out of poverty, and may you find more happiness than you ever thought possible as you collect enough money, enough friends, and enough meaning in your life to make you smile your way through the rest of your days.

What You Can Do Next

In this section you will find a compilation of ideas from this book that can be used to guide your next steps toward helping to end poverty in your community.

AFFORDABLE HOUSING

The cost of *housing* drives the tyranny of the moment for families struggling in poverty. You can:

- Get involved with city council sessions on housing. Find out what can be done to increase affordable housing and ask your council to pursue new strategies.
- Contact your congressional representatives and ask for information on what they are doing to increase affordable housing. Our federal government can and should play a larger role in making affordable housing a reality.
- Join your local Habitat for Humanity's efforts to build affordable homes.
- Find out if your community has a Community Land Trust program. If not, consider helping to start one.

AFFORDABLE TRANSPORTATION

Unless your community has public transportation that extends to all jobs during all shifts, people will need access to affordable cars. If your community already has a car donation program, consider donating your car next time you are ready to sell it, and talk your friends into doing it as well. If there is not one, you can go online and research "car donation programs" and "low-cost car purchase programs." Suggest implementing your favorite model in your community. Having an affordable car can literally transform a family's life.

FOOD AND COMMUNITY

In our town, a community meal is served at the local Methodist church every Monday, Tuesday, Thursday, Friday, and Sunday evening. At these events, sponsored by the congregation (who has come to realize that people in poverty are not "those people" but, rather, are people they want to get to know), you get both a meal and a community. Dinner friendships can be turned into something more whenever anyone wants that to happen. Your community may also provide other opportunities for getting to know those who are struggling to meet their basic needs.

BRIDGES OUT OF POVERTY

If your community has not yet brought in the *Bridges Out of Poverty* program, I highly recommend that you do so. This program will provide you and other community members with a powerful overview of why poverty exists, and what can be done about it. Move the Mountain has formed a strategic partnership with aha! Process, Inc. to link *Bridges Out of Poverty* with our Circles™ Campaign. Using these tools, your community can create a framework for the long-term goal of reducing and eventually ending poverty. Contact us at www.movethemountain.org for more information and help getting started.

BUILDING YOUR COMMUNITY'S CAPACITY TO ADDRESS POVERTY

In every community there are organizations dedicated to helping people in poverty. Almost without exception, these are unable to meet the demands created by high levels of poverty throughout the nation. To make the most of precious resources, Move the Mountain has developed the Transformational Planning and Leadership Program to assist organizations with maximizing their impact. We also designed the Circles approach to help people living comfortably build relationships with people who are struggling to meet their basic needs. These two strategies can be used together to dramatically increase the overall effectiveness of community efforts to help eradicate poverty. Our complementary programs are described in more detail below.

1. Move the Mountain Transformational Leadership & Planning (TLP) Program Description

Poverty can be solved if those of us who are leading the cause can shift from being effective managers of programs to effective transformational leaders who gain the full commitment of our community to the goal of ending poverty. The first step along the road to becoming an effective *transformational leader* is to develop a *leadership agenda* that will guide your actions in the community.

Once this agenda is in place, every meeting, every communication, and every event can be used as an opportunity to tell people why we must change, how things will be better once we change, and how the change can be accomplished.

A leadership agenda consists of the following three components:

- A description of the case for change that is compelling and urgent.
- A description of a preferred future that attractively presents how life could be.
- A description of primary strategies for how to get from here to there.

Without a compelling case for change, there is no urgency to move forward. Without an attractive preferred future, there is insufficient motivation to change at all. Without sound strategies, there is no practical way of implementing the dream. Once a leader articulates the leadership agenda, he or she can begin to gain the commitment of key stakeholders in the process of moving forward. Achieving the vision will be a communal experience, involving many groups of people.

The main task of leadership, then, is to align the community to the vision by articulating one's leadership agenda in every possible way, each and every day, until it is achieved.

Here is my own leadership agenda:

My mission is to inspire and equip community leaders to end poverty.

My case for change is:

- One-third of all households in the nation are unable to pay for their basic needs on a regular basis.
- Costs of all basic needs will rise in the next five years.
- Government support systems for people in poverty will likely continue to diminish in the next five years.
- Jobs will continue to become more competitive as more sectors are globalized.
- People in poverty are often isolated, leading to chronic depression and anxiety.

My preferred future is that:

- All families in our nation are able to meet their basic needs on a regular basis and experience stability.
- All children graduate from high school and have a realistic income plan for meeting their basic needs.
- Communities are free of poverty and related symptoms like crime and drug abuse.
- All families have not only enough money but also enough meaning and friendship in order to thrive.

My primary strategies are to (through our TLP programs):

- Inspire and equip community leaders to develop and pursue a transformational change agenda.

- Teach leaders how to move from low- to high-impact strategies that engage the community.
- Implement the high-impact strategy, the *Circles Campaign*, in communities across the country.
- Write books that inspire and equip ordinary people to do extraordinary things that contribute to ending poverty.

You can use my example to craft your own personal mission statement, case for change, preferred future, and strategies. Once you have a leadership agenda, the world opens up new opportunities to lead—and to make a difference in the lives of others.

2. Circles Campaign

Move the Mountain was initiated in 1992 by Mid-Iowa Community Action, the agency that had tested and promoted a self-sufficiency program model called Family Development. Starting the Circles Campaign to create partnerships among individual volunteers ("allies") and families pursuing economic well-being ("leaders"), with the larger goal of ending poverty in their communities, was the next evolutionary step. Circles systematically support participants in learning to have enough money, meaning, and friendship.

Circles Campaigns have three primary goals:

- Invite the community to join with the social services system to help people get out of poverty.
- Inspire and equip the community to eradicate poverty.
- Facilitate development of genuine, lasting relationships among individuals from different backgrounds and walks of life for the purpose of informing and supporting low-income earners as they take steps toward making a permanent move out of poverty.

Getting prepared for bringing a Circles Campaign to your community:

You can begin your preparation in the following ways:

- Review the rest of this section for more information about the Circles model and other Move the Mountain training resources.
- Visit our website, www.movethemountain.org.
- Review the aha! Process website, www.ahaprocess.com, for background information on *Bridges Out of Poverty* and *Getting Ahead in a Just-Getting'-By World.* Read the books and purchase the curriculum materials to help members of your community prepare for participating in a Circles Campaign.
- Attend a *Bridges Out of Poverty* training session.
- Begin establishing connections with like-minded people and organizations in your community who might join you in supporting a Circles Campaign.

3. Transformational Leadership and Strategic Planning Program

- How do anti-poverty agencies effectively return to their mission of ending poverty?
- In times of shrinking government funding, how can community organizations redirect their time and resources in order to actually increase opportunities for livable-wage jobs, affordable housing, adequate healthcare, and reliable transportation?
- How do community organizations engage more citizens in helping families out of poverty?
- How do community organizations transform low-impact strategies into high-impact ones?

With funding from the federal government's Office of Community Services and a decade of R & D (research and development) funding from the Annie E. Casey Foundation, the Move the Mountain Leadership Center has developed the Transformational Leadership and Strategic Planning Program to help community organizations increase their capacity to reduce poverty today and lay the groundwork for eventually ending it. Our 10-step process builds on strong techniques available from leadership and strategic-planning programs, from both the private and public sectors, which can guide your community organization toward playing a more powerful role in dismantling poverty.

Contact us today at www.movethemountain.org to get started with bringing these initiatives to your community.

About the Author

MY OWN STORY AND MOVE THE MOUNTAIN LEADERSHIP CENTER'S APPROACH TO CIRCLES™

Having been academically successful all my life, I entered an Honors College after finishing high school with high hopes of becoming an architect, planning in this way to realize long-held assumptions of what my future would hold. During the course of my first year there it became abundantly clear that, for a variety of reasons, I was not going to be able to continue on that path. Recognizing that I was facing one of life's crossroads, a good friend suggested that I spend the first summer of my college career volunteering at the Catholic Worker House in downtown Rochester, New York.

I had been raised in the relatively affluent suburban town of Fairport, 10 miles outside the city. I had never in my life been in close contact with people living in poverty. Since I was anxiously searching for direction, I thought, "Why not give it a try? What have I got to lose?"

Like millions in the United States, I had always been so involved with my comfortably affluent world that the daily realities confronted by those in poverty had never entered my mind. After the first week at the Worker House, I wondered, "How could there be this much poverty so close to me—and yet I never saw it, thought about it, *or* cared about it before?"

After letting go of any lingering ideas about becoming an architect, I went about getting my bachelor's degree in Business Administration with a major in Organizational Behavior, then went straight into social work. The divine logic of my circuitous path would eventually make itself known. Knowledge of the design features of architecture, the pragmatics of business structure, and theories of organizational behavior would combine with the compassion

I gained during my emotionally challenging, abrupt change in life's direction to ultimately serve me well in the journey that lay ahead of me.

My first job as a paid social services worker was with Catholic Charities. I was hired to run the emergency financial assistance program. I was informed that I had $1,000 to help families in severe financial distress—those experiencing evictions, utility shut-offs, and a variety of other bad situations. Being raised in a comfortable home where there was always plenty of money to solve such problems, I thought my superiors meant $1,000 for every person. No, *that was the entire month's budget,* and I would see somewhere between 30 and 40 families every week! I was shocked, not only by the total inadequacy of available funding, but also by how the very good people who ran the place had apparently become so resigned to the situation that such an anemic response to helping fellow humans meet basic survival needs had been normalized.

A few months into the job, I and several hundred other people from across the state of Ohio working in the emergency assistance business attended a conference. I realized there that experiences I was having in my job were the norm in our business. I was an *isolated* worker trying to help a parade of people *isolated by poverty,* with such inadequate resources that dealing with situations analogous to using a squirt gun to put out a house fire had simply become the daily routine.

Through a serendipitous conversation with a stranger at a cocktail party one evening, I was encouraged to go a foundation in Cleveland to request a grant to do something about what I was seeing. His contact at the foundation liked my ideas. She sent me to another foundation for matching funds. I ultimately managed to secure a total of $23,000 from three foundations for the purpose of building a network to address emergency assistance issues. With that first grant success, more than 100 people joined me to talk about what we as a group could do to better address poverty. Near Lake Erie at the time the only get-out-of-poverty project around was the "give-people-bus-passes-out-of-town" program, since the unemployment rate was so high. No one was really helping people out of poverty. Instead, immediate but temporary assistance was provided. We were a motivated group looking for good, concrete ideas.

FAMILY DEVELOPMENT ORGANIZATION

At that time, Gary Stokes was the director of Mid-Iowa Community Action, Inc. (MICA), an anti-poverty agency based in Marshalltown, Iowa. He came to Columbus, Ohio, in 1985 to talk about a new approach to poverty he and his colleagues were organizing called Family Development. Back in Iowa, they had talked with thousands of families they had served during the previous years to find out how many people had successfully moved out of poverty. They were making an attempt to understand which of their many programs had been most helpful. To their great dismay, only a small percentage had risen above the poverty level—and most of those because they had married someone with a job! Gary and his colleagues decided that in order to be more effective they needed to get out from behind their desks to meet people in their homes, getting to know them in order to help with achieving goals that would lead to self-sufficiency.

I loved this idea. Gary and I talked about organizing the same kinds of programs across Ohio. Over the next five years, with Gary's coaching, I set up a nonprofit known as the Ohio Center for Family Development. We started projects in Cleveland, Akron, Canton, Cincinnati, and Columbus. Doors were opened to us by more than 50 foundations and United Way chapters that recognized the efficacy of getting intentional about helping families out of poverty. We first raised a couple of million dollars to test the initiative. At the apex of our initial capacity, we had 50 family development specialists working out of 38 different agencies, and we touched the lives of hundreds of families. For most of that time this was a thrilling challenge. Then the innovation money ran out as the state of Ohio entered into one of its bleak budget-deficit spells. The ideas seeded by Family Development had become embedded in some organizations in Cleveland and Columbus thanks to key foundations and community leaders, but they pretty much died away in Canton, most of Akron, and Cincinnati.

By the fourth year of incorporation, I no longer liked the job I had created for myself. I was feeling too isolated, so I mentioned to Gary I was interested in working with his team. Gary called me a couple of weeks later and offered me a job to be funded by a new grant he had received from the federal government. I was to help him organize a one-day event in which thousands of people would have small-group dialogues about what the community wanted for its families in the future. He had been having conversations with a program officer from the Annie E. Casey Foundation and was hopeful that we would receive a grant from the foundation. With his customary confidence, he said, "Come out to Iowa."

So my wife and I gathered up our belongings, bundled up our cat, and moved to Marshalltown, Iowa, which was a two-company town—the original home of Fisher Controls and the Lennox Furnace Company. In January 1992 I was the newcomer to a bright and initially somewhat intimidating team of top managers at MICA. Unlike myself, many of the MICA managers held advanced degrees and had excellent writing skills. Nevertheless, within a few weeks I found my way and began to feel like I would become a contributing member of Gary's team.

During my first months in Iowa, I helped the MICA team gather people in churches, homes, and community centers on one April evening to watch a video that would guide them through a dialogue. To my amazement, we succeeded in having more than 7,000 people participate! A communitywide plan emerged to help us direct our activities for the next five years. We secured a $260,000/year, five-year grant from the Casey Foundation to work with education and human service leaders in our five-county region to develop strategic plans and collaborations that would help to fulfill this new vision. Gary named this work *Move the Mountain.*

MOVE THE MOUNTAIN ORGANIZATION

The first two years of Move the Mountain were energizing. I was full of hope because we had 56 leaders of the health, human service, and education systems actively involved in Move the Mountain. But by 1994 many of those same 56 leaders had become the source of my growing discontent. Our discussions were too focused on budgets, buildings, and plans. It seemed to me that the people we served tended to be viewed as distant objects or conversation pieces. To remedy this, I started meeting with more "grassroots" folks in Ames to try to determine a new direction. In late 1994 I wrote a successful planning grant for state funds that would allow us to bring together low-income people with other concerned citizens into a series of community sessions for the purpose of helping to strengthen families. Using these funds we organized evening meetings among more than 30 people who lived at the poverty level and another 60 people from the middle-income level. Community teams were formed: People in poverty joined people who weren't in poverty to discuss solutions to affordable housing, affordable childcare, and the problems that arise when families become too isolated.

I wrote another grant to start a support group for low-income people who wanted to become leaders for our community team meetings. This grant application was inspired by an amazing woman, Lois Smidt, a tenant farmer's daughter from northern Iowa with a big heart, a good mind, *and* ... an advanced degree in English. She had powerful ideas about how to build relationships to address not only economic privilege, but also other divisive stereotyping cultural attitudes, such as racism, sexism, and ageism.

Lois took me to a series of workshops led by facilitators from the international group known as Re-evaluation Counseling, also referred to as "co-counseling." There I learned tools for building relationships with those in different economic circumstances, including ways to dismantle distress patterns that kept me from getting as close to others as I could. One of this group's goals was the elimination of poverty. Even though I was working in a community action agency that had a federal mandate to end poverty, I had never before heard anyone articulate the idea as an intentional goal. I challenged our local steering committee to set the goal of ending poverty in our county in our lifetime. Negotiating a lot of challenging changes during college gave me the advantage of making every new external problem since then seem eminently doable. What could possibly stop us from ending poverty? We had developed successful Social Security, suffrage, and civil rights movements—and had landed a man on the moon! We *could* end poverty *if* we wanted to.

BEYOND WELFARE ORGANIZATION

By 1996 Lois and I had launched Beyond Welfare. We were committed to ending poverty in Story County by helping families get off welfare with the help of caring individuals from the middle economic level in peer support groups. When two retired men from the Episcopal Church approached us to ask how they could help Beyond Welfare, we suggested that they find some cars, since something everyone in our group was having problems with was transportation. The men were successful! This became one of the initial incentives for encouraging people to move out of isolation—to join our weekly meetings, build new friendships, and develop plans for future economic well-being. From 1997 to 2004, Beyond Welfare transferred 160 cars to families so they could get to work or college. During that time, with Beyond Welfare's help, 52 families increased their income by an average of more than $1,100/month and left welfare.

CIRCLES

In the summer of 2000 I attended a weeklong training program on community organizing at Ghost Ranch in New Mexico. During this program John McKnight (the well-known author of *Building Communities from the Inside Out* and other books) and his colleagues shared their insights about associational life and the folly of turning all the problems of poverty over to established social service agencies. Their premise was that each community must take on responsibility for helping its own members. The lead trainer, Mike Green, helped to place Move the Mountain into its Assets Based Community Development national network, and for the next two years we enjoyed quarterly site visits from him. Mike told us about an idea he called "Circles of Support" that had been used in Canada to help keep disabled people out of institutionalized living.

Through Beyond Welfare, well-intentioned people were matched with families trying to get out of poverty in one-to-one relationships we called "family partners." This approach worked somewhat, but a lot of family partners burned out, mostly because of isolation. I translated the Circles approach in my mind for use as an alternative to family partners. We could recruit two or three people with middle-level incomes to work together as allies with one person or family struggling to solve a problem, thereby reducing isolation and pressure for any one individual.

Thus began the Circles initiative in Ames, Iowa. As allies, we could now share our successes and failures while traversing the often messy trail of building relationships to overcome problems stemming from being raised in very different circumstances.

I was so excited I began talking about Circles with everyone, everywhere I went. We had a federal grant to present transformational leadership development for community action executives in eight states. This seemed like a good opportunity to talk about Circles. I had a contract to develop grassroots leadership in Des Moines; it seemed important to talk about Circles here too. The state of Iowa gave us a grant to expand Beyond Welfare. Again, we talked about Circles. The concept of Circles proved to be something that people could easily understand and relate to. Although the business of helping someone out of poverty is complex, the simplicity of using a Circle to tackle this challenge is elegant and inviting.

I myself joined two Circles and found they were a great use of my time. I helped those in need of support as I helped those who, like me, needed and wanted to give back to others. In the process I experienced tremendous satisfaction from not spending extra money and time on trivial pursuits that would only have left me feeling empty—when I was making a growing difference in the lives of my neighbors instead. Circles were capturing more and more attention as some version of them was launched in 22 communities in Arizona, California, Iowa, Minnesota, and Missouri.

The Kellogg Foundation awarded Beyond Welfare a special grant of $100,000/year for three years to research and document its processes so that other communities could learn from it. The State of Iowa approached us to adapt Circles to help former felons reconnect with community life. We also received contracts from Minnesota and Missouri to provide more formalized training about the Circles approach to their community action agencies. Although we were still "babes in the woods," by then we had created a rich community of fellow students learning together about how to engage organizations and several levels of government in the task of helping families out of poverty. Today we have community leaders developing Circles Campaigns in Connecticut, Pennsylvania, Ohio, Indiana, Idaho, Missouri, Minnesota, and New Mexico.

The Circles Campaign has become a community organizing tool, as well as an empowerment tool. Even with the recognition of the strength of Circles, however, there are many other strategies we must pursue to end poverty. For example, we need to create:

- More roadmaps for ending poverty because people are unique individuals having differing responses to various plans
- More imaginative economic development
- Campaigns for 100% graduation rates from high schools, resulting in competent graduates who are ready to enter the workforce
- More community leadership development
- Fair and equitable tax reforms
- Development of more sustainable food and housing initiatives

We invite you to create a Circles Campaign in your own community. Circles put a face on poverty and bring the pain it causes closer to people who have plenty of money. Circles are an invitation to become more generous, aware, and connected. Circles are a means to achieve healthier, more vibrant communities, with less crime, drug abuse, racism, and other forms of oppression.

We can and we should end poverty in this nation—and help other nations do the same. It is not simply the right thing to do: It is the next imperative step to take to sustain the human race on Mother Earth.

Bibliography

Bach, David. (2005). *The Automatic Millionaire: A Powerful One-Step Plan to Live and Finish Rich.* New York, NY: Broadway.

CACI International. 1100 N. Glebe Road, Arlington, VA 22201. Personal communication.

Chatzky, Jean. (2003). *You Don't Have to Be Rich: Comfort, Happiness, and Financial Security on Your Own Terms.* New York, NY: Portfolio.

DeVol, Phillip. (2004). *Getting Ahead in a Just-Getting'-By World.* Highlands, TX: aha! Process.

DeVol, Philip E., Payne, Ruby K., & Smith, Terie Dreussi. (2006). *Bridges Out of Poverty* (Fourth Edition). Highlands, TX: aha! Process.

Dominguez, Joe, & Robin, Vicki. (1992). *Your Money or Your Life: Transforming Your Relationship with Money and Achieving Financial Independence.* New York, NY: Viking Adult.

Freedman, Jonathan. (1978). *Happy People: What Happiness Is, Who Has It, and Why.* San Diego, CA: Harcourt Brace Jovanovich.

Green, Mike, Moore, Henry, & O'Brien, John. (2006). *ABCD in Action: When People Care Enough to Act.* Toronto, Ontario, Canada: Inclusion Press.

Hacker, Andrew. (1997). *Money: Who Has How Much and Why.* New York, NY: Scribner.

Kretzmann, John P., & McKnight, John L. (1997). *Building Communities from the Inside Out: A Path Toward Finding and Mobilizing a Community's Assets.* Skokie, IL: ACTA Publications.

Mather, Anne. *All-Consuming Passion: Waking Up from the American Dream* (Second Edition). (1993). Seattle, WA: New Road Map Foundation. Also available at www.ecofuture.org/pk/pkar9506.html

Mid-Iowa Community Action. © 1996 Mid-Iowa Community Action. Marshalltown, IA. Research conducted internally. www.micaonline.org

Miller, Scott C. (April 10, 2000). *Ames Tribune,* Ames, IA. Eliminating poverty in Story County.

Miller, Scott C. (May 18, 2000). *Ames Tribune.* Poverty filled with single moms.

Miller, Scott C. (July 17, 2000). *Ames Tribune.* Housing is key to reducing poverty.

Miller, Scott C. (October 17, 2000). *Ames Tribune.* Child-care aid is needed.

Miller, Scott C. (December 27, 2001). *Ames Tribune.* Help people out of isolation.

Miller, Scott C. (2006). Move the Mountain: A Transformational Planning Guide. Ames, IA: Move the Mountain Leadership Center.

Payne, Ruby K. (2006). *A Framework for Understanding Poverty* (Fifth Edition). Highlands, TX: aha! Process.

ON THE INTERNET

Bennett, Jessica. Q/A: Why consumer debt is rising: An economist talks about the scope of America's growing consumer debt, what's behind it and what it means for the future. *Newsweek:MSNBC.com web exclusive.* (August 8, 2006). Accessed May 13, 2007. blogs.ocregister.com/lansner/archives/2006/12/tell_us_hows_the_fed_doing.html

Berlin, Gordon L. Congressional testimony by Gordon Berlin on solutions to poverty. *Manpower Research Development Corporation.* (April 26, 2007). Accessed May 13, 2007. www.mdrc.org/publications/450/testimony.html

Environmental Defense. Fight global warming. *Environmental Defense.* (2007). Accessed 13 May 2007. www.fightglobalwarming.com/index.cfm

Global Footprint Network. Ecological footprint: Overview. *Global Footprint Network.* (2003–07). Accessed April 29, 2007. www.footprintnetwork.org/gfn_sub.php?content=footprint_overview

Mihelich, Peggy, & Williams, David E. Scientists: humans 'very likely' cause global warming. *CNN.* (April 29, 2007). Accessed April 29, 2007. www.cnn.com/2007/TECH/science/02/02/climate.change.report/index.html

National Association of Home Builders. New home size reaches all-time high in 2005. *National Association of Home Builders.* (June 26, 2006). Accessed May 13, 2007. www.nahb.org/news_details.aspx?newsID=2847

New American Dream. Hot holiday gift for kids this year? A piggy bank, say fed-up Americans—materialism, high cost of living has public focusing on more meaningful holiday, new poll reveals. *New American Dream.* (Holiday Poll Archive: 2005.) Accessed May 13, 2007. www.newdream.org/holiday/poll05.php

Recommended Reading

U.S. Census Bureau. Archives. *U.S. Census Bureau* (including April 2007). Accessed April 2007. www.census.gov

Barndt, Joseph R. (1991). *Dismantling Racism.* Minneapolis, MN: Augsburg Fortress.

Blix, Jacqueline, & Heitmiller, David. (1997). *Getting a Life: Strategies for Simple Living.* New York, NY: Penguin Books.

Green, Mike, with Moore, Henry, & Obrien, John. (2007). *ABCD in Action: When People Care Enough To Act.* Toronto, Ontario: Inclusion Press.

Grisham, Vaughn L. Jr. (1999). *Tupelo: the Evolution of a Community.* Dayton, OH: The Kettering Foundation Press.

Homan, Fr. Daniel, OSB, & Pratt, Lonni Collins. (2002). *Radical Hospitality: Benedict's Way of Love.* Brewster, MA: Paraclete Press.

Lopez, Ian F. Haney. (1996). *White by Law: The Legal Construction of Race.* New York, NY: NYU Press.

Lorrance, Arleen. (1972). *The Love Project.* San Diego, CA: LP Publications.

Muller, Wayne. (1999). *Sabbath: Finding Rest, Renewal, and Delight in Our Busy Lives.* New York, NY: Bantam Books.

Phillips, Kevin. (2002). *Wealth and Democracy: a Political History of the United States.* New York, NY: Broadway Books.

Pierce, Linda Breen. (2000). *Choosing Simplicity: Real People Finding Peace and Fulfillment in a Complex World.* Carmel, CA: Gallagher Press.

Pike, Diane Kennedy, as Paulus, Mariamne. (2003). *Awakening to Wisdom.* Scottsdale, AZ: Teleos Imprint.

Seligman, Martin E.P. (2002). *Authentic Happiness: Using the New Positive Psychology to Realize your Potential for Lasting Fulfillment.* New York, NY: Free Press.

Tolle, Eckhart. (2005). *A New Earth: Awakening to Your Life's Purpose.* New York, NY: Penguin Books.

- Join our **aha!** news list

  Receive our free newsletter with periodic news, updates, recent articles by Dr. Ruby K. Payne, and more!

- Register online for Bridges Out of Poverty U.S. National Tour and Dr. Payne's U.S. National Tour

- Visit our online store

  Books, videos, workshops

- Learn about our Training Certification programs

  A Framework for Understanding Poverty

  Bridges Out of Poverty

  Meeting Standards & Raising Test Scores

- If you liked *Until It's Gone,* look for *Bridges Out of Poverty* and *Getting Ahead in a Just-Gettin'-By World: Building Your Resources for a Better Life,* a step-by-step life-planning workbook for individuals in poverty working in groups with a facilitator.

Order Form

Please send me _____ copy/copies of *Until It's Gone* at $14.95 per book (or $11.95 each for 5 or more books). Enclosed is payment for:

Books	$ ____________	
Shipping	$ ____________	($4.50 first book + $2.00 each additional book)
Subtotal	$ ____________	
Sales tax	$ ____________	(Only residents of Alabama, Florida, Georgia, Kentucky, Nebraska, New Mexico, Tennessee, and Texas)
Total	$ ____________	

UPS Ship-to Address (no post office boxes, please)

Name ______________________________

Organization ______________________________

Address ______________________________

____

Phone ______________________________

E-mail ______________________________

Method of Payment

PO # ______________________________

Credit card type ______________ Exp. ______________

Credit card # ______________________________

Check $ ______________ Check # ______________

Thanks for your order!

www.ahaprocess.com

PO Box 727 • Highlands, TX 77562-0727
(800) 424-9484 • fax (281) 426-5600